The Real Enemy

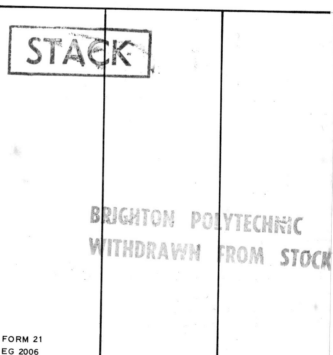

The Real Enemy

Pierre d'Harcourt

Longmans

LONGMANS, GREEN AND CO LTD
48 Grosvenor Street, London W1
*Associated companies, branches and representatives
throughout the world*

© *Pierre d'Harcourt 1967*
First published 1967

Printed in Great Britain by
The Camelot Press Ltd, London and Southampton

*'To my children
in memory of all those who died
hoping that their sacrifice
would not be useless'*

Part One

I

I am French. My earliest ancestors came from Denmark, and bore such names as Torf and Turchetil. They settled in Normandy, and their descendants took part in the invasion of England with William the Conqueror. Some remained there and became the English Harcourts.

At the battle of Agincourt there was a Harcourt in each camp.

My family has produced marshals, admirals, academicians (my father was the last), scholars and ambassadors. But also countrymen—huntsmen and fishermen—generally cultivated and intelligent; and a few humbly devoted priests. Very few were courtiers; mostly they eschewed luxury, were of independent spirit and loved books. One among them was a great gardener. This was the Duc d'Harcourt of just before the French Revolution. He wrote a book on landscape gardening which I am told is still authoritative.

The link with England was renewed during the Revolution when the English Harcourts sheltered their *émigré* cousins.

Just before the Second World War the King of England visited France. An Admiral d'Harcourt commanded the vessels which escorted him, General d'Harcourt led the aeroplanes which flew over his procession, and Colonel d'Harcourt, with his Spahis, accompanied the King into Paris.

In my father the usual family tendency to behave stubbornly about values strongly believed in was accentuated by the accident of poor eyesight—in fact it led to his future career. One day, when he was still a small boy, he saw some troops exercising in the fields not far from the house. He ran home in great excitement to tell his parents about it. The army, after all, was the family career. His mother hurt him deeply by saying, 'Don't make yourself ridiculous—no one as blind as you ever got into the army.' My father never got over that, and as a direct result in his early teens he left home and began a series of wanderings around Europe. He had a small inheritance of his own, and as he went from one university to another he developed a particular knowledge of German politics and culture which became the basis of his reputation for German scholarship in France. He grew to be an expert on Goethe and Schiller, and at the outbreak of the Second World War he was Professor of German literature. He was also one of the first and most outspoken critics of National Socialism. Since 1932 he had a very clear vision of what was going to happen. He had many close friends among the leading German Catholic Democrats and wrote numerous books which, though affectionate towards the German people, were extremely critical of the Nazi régime.

It was when I was with my father that I first became clearly aware of what Nazism meant. We were at Innsbruck on the evening before Dolfüss was murdered, dining with the Chief of Police of Vienna, whom my father knew well. The next day our host was shot in the streets. I remember feeling then that something terrible had come upon us. That night on the mountain slopes, on the side of the river nearest to Germany, the local Nazis built an enormous fiery swastika. An hour later on our side the Cross of Christ was burning. The two flaming symbols confronted each other across the valley and I knew that they were the symbols of the conflict that was to come.

When the war broke out I had already been called up and was in a famous cavalry regiment whose horses had been exchanged for motor-cycles. As luck would have it I was on leave in Paris in that beautiful summer weather of 1940 when the big German offensive began. My unit had been stationed near Calais when I left, so I returned as quickly as I could. It was a few days before Dunkirk fell. We took up a defensive position alongside a British anti-aircraft unit which seemed to be entirely on its own, and set up our machine-guns in front of a massive old coastal fort. Its guns, needless to say, were all pointing in the opposite direction from the oncoming German tanks. The fort was heavily shelled, but we were protected down on the sands in front. I suppose I helped to loose off a couple of hundred rounds, until sand jammed the mechanism. Even if we had hit a tank we could not possibly have damaged it, but we felt that nevertheless we should try. When the heavy shelling stopped to let the German tanks and armoured cars through, we were ordered to fall back on to the fort. Several of my companions were killed, for in climbing up the slope to it we naturally made good targets.

I suppose this little resistance effort of ours lasted about two days. At the end of it a handful of us, worn out and half-starved, made for the town. We decided to take refuge individually or in twos and threes in private houses. The Germans were still shooting in the streets at anything suspicious and one of my companions was shot dead a few feet away from me. The people of Calais were terrified at the thought of protracted street fighting and in the house where I took shelter there were several frightened little children. Surrender seemed the responsible course. So, when I saw some approaching Germans who did not look too trigger-happy, I stepped out into the street with my hands well above my head and asked as courteously as possible to be captured.

Everything was very casual. A number of us were told to get into a lorry and were driven slowly along to some intended destination. The lorry slowed down and stopped several times and was almost completely unguarded. Now that all the firing had ceased and things were settling down there seemed less point in being a prisoner, so I stepped off the lorry at a convenient corner and liberated myself. Walking away at a reasonable pace, almost the first building I saw was a hospital. It was full of wounded and obviously very short of staff, so I went to the commanding officer and told him who and what I was. In a few minutes my army papers had been altered and I was registered as an army nurse.

There were three wounded British officers in the hospital and I thought that in due course I might be able to escape to England with them. But when news came that the hospital unit was to be moved—possibly to Germany—I thought it would be wiser to leave immediately, and by myself, while the going was good. I decided to aim for my family home near Reims, about two hundred miles away. I set off wearing ordinary blue workman's overalls and had with me a large piece of stale bread, and some tobacco which I hoped to exchange for food on the way. Here and there I begged a glass of milk or a glass of wine. People were very nice to me and as it was fine midsummer weather the journey was not too arduous.

At Amiens I discovered that the Germans were inundated with French prisoners and were sending them home as quickly as possible. All I had to do was to file along with many others in front of a German sergeant, who merely looked at us, glanced at our papers and gave us an official demobilisation form which stated that it was all right for us to be at large.

I still had to walk home. As vividly as if it were yesterday I remember the last few strides up to the top of the hill from which I would see my home, a mile away down in the valley, the roof showing here and there between the leafy trees. Until this moment, in spite of what had happened, I had lived in a world which though abnormal was still one I recognised. I was walking out of that world for ever as I climbed the hill. There was my home, but on the flagpole which rose clear from the trees flew a Nazi flag. I was amazed and horrified by the speed with which the Germans had got there and extremely anxious about my parents, for I knew that my father was on the Nazi black list because of the books he had written about them. To proceed straight to the house would have been dangerous, so I took a round-about way through the wooded by-lanes. As I was cautiously approaching the house from the back I caught sight of the village carpenter. He had always disapproved of me and my family; as a communist sympathiser he classified us as filthy

4

capitalists and gentry. We had always regarded him as hostile and if ever I saw him in the street I pretended not to notice him. Now it was different. As soon as he saw me he ran to meet me. My father and mother were in hiding, he said, and the house was full of Germans. He insisted on taking me back to his house and feeding me. The old world was changing fast.

To escape the eye of the occupying Germans would have been impossible and, unless there were a good reason for doing so, it was not worth the attempt. They were extremely thorough. Once they had come into the village, they took stock of every item, every field and wood, every cock and hen, every apple tree, as William the Conqueror had done for England in the *Domesday Book*. They were efficient organisers and put everybody to work. The elderly local farmer was made to drive his own tractor and his daughter, who had never worked in her life, was made to do clerical work in the German headquarters. My own record was not anti-German; I had no idea where my parents were; and I was in possession of perfectly respectable demobilisation papers. I decided not to conceal myself but to behave normally. It would only be a day or two anyway before they knew of my whereabouts.

My immediate objective, now that I knew my parents were alive and presumably safe, was to ensure that my father had left no material behind him which might incriminate him. I went to the German officer in charge of the village and obtained permission to go into the house on the pretext of getting a change of clothes and collecting a few personal belongings. A few not very attentive guards accompanied me and I went through the rooms of our home picking up obvious things, clothes, trinkets and a family picture or two. While I moved from one room to another, the guards hung about, paying less and less attention as the hours wore on, and I was able to collect my father's papers. I did not risk valuable time trying to dispose of them there and then, but I filled my pockets with them, took them back to the village and gave them to a friend who burned them after I had left.

Now, in search of my parents, I headed for Reims, and the headquarters of Veuve-Clicquot, the family champagne business.

Here I stayed with my uncle, Jean de Caraman Chimay, until news arrived from my mother. He, his wife and I camped in the offices of the firm, and one evening my uncle wrapped himself in the Union Jack (saved from the Consulate, where another uncle had been British Consul), and proclaimed the three of us 'Résistants!'

When the Germans broke through and rushed on Paris, my mother had fled from Reims. The car broke down near Cheverny, where she was now hiding, and she had written to my uncle— indirectly through trusted friends—for news and money. But we still heard nothing from my father. I felt it would be advisable to get rid of any incriminating papers in the flat in Paris, so when my uncle said that he had obtained a permit to drive there I decided to go with him.

Paris was now a strange, frightening and empty city. Three-quarters of its inhabitants were on the roads somewhere spread across the countryside. I went straight to the flat, feeling that there might be no time to lose. I was right. The Gestapo arrived first thing next morning, having been informed by the concierge that a member of the d'Harcourt family was on the premises. He had nothing against us, but he feared what would happen to him if he did not report and my presence was discovered. His attitude was typical at that moment in Paris. But by the time the Gestapo arrived I had disposed of all the papers. They questioned me at length about my parents but eventually went away.

The atmosphere in France in those early days of the German occupation was extraordinary—and unhealthy. The air was full of fear and of the face-saving feeling that after all France was still a country. Was there not a government of France in Vichy? Anyone who behaved as though France were still at war was not merely a dangerous fool but something worse, some kind of traitor. The allegation of treachery was necessary to enable people to work up enough indignation to stifle their feelings of guilt at being so demoralised.

In Vichy, where I now went, it was even worse. Having

6

heard that my father had arrived there, I followed him. The atmosphere was one of fear, corruption and intrigue. It would have been quite unnerving had it not been for my father, whose integrity and resolution shone brightly against this dark setting.

People at Vichy could be divided into three groups. There were those, like my father, who wanted to do what they could to save France and were determined to collaborate as little as possible with the Germans. They were a small minority. A second group, also fairly small, had decided that it was in the best interests of France to collaborate with the victorious enemy. Some of these were sincere and good men, others were cowardly and self-seeking. Then there was a third and much larger group of people who did not know quite what to think or say. Some were genuinely torn in mind about what to do; others did not dare to think clearly in case the conclusions they came to would be too dangerous for them or their relations and friends.

My own mind was clear. I would continue the fight against Hitler, although I did not know quite how this was to be done. The opportunity fortunately presented itself when a young lieutenant in charge of demobilisation formally interviewed me about where I had been when France surrendered, how I had got there, whom I was with and so on. He seemed particularly interested in what I told him about the fall of Calais. He also wanted to know what I proposed to do now and what I would have been doing if the war had not come. I said that I would be studying in Paris and that if I did the normal thing I would go back to resume my course. He spoke very guardedly but said he would like me to talk to his superior officer, Captain Simoneau.

In the next week or two I met Simoneau several times. Eventually he came out with:

'Would you like to do some work for us? It's a rather special kind of work. An organisation of ours is starting up in Paris collecting information. There's a major in charge of it there and I think you could help him.'

I told him I would like to do this provided that the information was going to assist in the effort to free France and damage the

7

Germans, and would not just be pigeon-holed in Vichy. This was a blunt statement to make to somebody of whom one was still not sure, but he responded with an even blunter one.

'The kind of information you would help us to get won't be pigeon-holed here,' he said. 'You can be sure that it will be passed on to others who could use it.'

This was very important. Simoneau was after all an officer in the French Army and ultimately responsible to the official government of France—the Vichy régime which had formally declared itself at peace with the Nazis. Whatever information came to Simoneau as an intelligence officer would be passed to the espionage department, known as Le Deuxième Bureau, at Vichy. But what he was saying was that, although it would be passed on, 'others' would have access to it, and these 'others' would be outside the collaborating régime and able and willing to go on resisting.

I undertook to go back to Paris and send information which would come back to Vichy and, if Simoneau was genuine, would also be passed on to those who could use it against the Germans. Whether this was to be from the safety of Britain or from inside France itself I did not gather and was not expected to enquire. In fact Simoneau was already recruiting suitable men to serve the underground organisation in unoccupied France.

Before returning to Paris to resume my studies I was to receive tuition in the elements of espionage from a Doctor Beaumaine in Vichy. Raoul Beaumaine was a wonderful character and if I had not seen and heard it with my own eyes I would find what I have to say about him quite incredible. Spies are supposed above all to be quiet, inconspicuous, part of the background. Beaumaine was a big, noisy, flash, theatrical character who went from pub to pub regaling the company with such remarks as: 'These bloody Germans. I'm now told they think I'm a spy.' He was always smartly, if not ostentatiously dressed, with many gold rings, wristlets and elegant shirts. He was a Belgian who had married a Canadian and was in peacetime a representative of a well-known champagne firm. He had lost an eye in the First World War and had now become very fat. He knew nothing of medicine but had an office with a doctor's plate outside. People came and went all day and presumably it was thought they were patients. They were in fact spies. Any set-up looking less like a doctor's practice and more like an espionage centre it would be hard to imagine. His main port of call was a bar called 'The Cintra', the haunt of the spies and agents, and as publicly associated with them as, say, El Vino's in Fleet Street is associated with journalists. He saw all information that ever came to the Deuxième Bureau or ever left it. He passed 'outside' whatever took his fancy to his connection in Switzerland, who then sent it to England.

At Beaumaine's flat I learned a number of skills, from comparatively laborious and complex things, such as how to use codes and how to recognise and describe the different units of the German Army, to simple things such as how to mix and use invisible ink.

I was very glad when the time came to return to Paris. Vichy was sickening. It was good to find a few men willing and equipping themselves to fight back, but in the nature of things I was allowed to meet very few. One could not be sure of how genuine these were. There was no means of telling, beyond one's own instinct and judgement.

In these days names like 'de Gaulle' meant very little if they were known at all. Terms like 'Underground' and 'Resistance Movement' had not been invented because the things themselves either did not exist or were not known to exist. It was all risky, tentative, shadowy, insubstantial. There was no group, body or institution to which one could turn. As antidotes to one's loneliness and the sense of being in a dangerous darkness, one relied for one's hopes on a few individuals one had known only for a day or two.

Apart from this the only thing that encouraged me was, paradoxically, the thing that depressed me most, the Church service on Sunday morning. With everything in turmoil after the débâcle, with no theatres, cinemas or concerts in Vichy, Sunday

9

morning service and church parade was the big social event of the week. Marshal Pétain would appear in full uniform; his guard of honour would roar up on motor-cycles; his staff would wear a breastful of medals; and civilian members of the government would wear top hats. It was laughable and tragic to see how Vichy France tried to keep up its self-respect and morale. It was all so enormously remote, childish and artificial. But it increased my desire to *do* something and, when the time came, it was with relief that I mounted my bicycle and rode to the border, along with many other refugees who had decided that it was now safe to return to Paris. There was no trouble with the border police and I set off for the capital with a sense of purpose.

2

My working name was to be Richard. My instructions were to go to a boulevard café called the Richelieu at a certain time on the morning of a certain day and sit there reading a certain newspaper. A man came up to me, sat down, ordered coffee, began to chat, gave the password and I knew it was my contact. It all was so much the way it is in books and on television that one almost had to laugh. A few days later I had a note telling me to go to an address in the rue de Trévise.

When I went up to the top of the stairs and opened the door I thought at first I had made a mistake. The room was full of people, clowns, ballet dancers, jugglers and acrobats applying for jobs. It was a theatrical agency. The sight of this room would have been comic enough at any time, but seen in connection with an espionage network it seemed absolutely ludicrous. Beyond the first suite of offices, however, was a second one, and this was where the information was collected. The blind was a magnificent protection, because in fact it was not a blind at all. Genuine clowns and chorus girls were in and out all day obtaining genuine engagements from a genuine impresario. The disguise was excellent. I remember a ridiculous face mask with a *képi* on top hanging on a hook on the wall. It was perfectly in keeping with the scene, but in the lining of the *képi* were the code names and addresses of several active agents. The theory of the professional spy who ran this extraordinary centre was that the more open your activities were the less you would be suspected. He was never caught, so his theory seemed sound.

This was the Major d'Autrevaux I had been told to report to. He was a very brave man. He sat day after day at the centre of these activities presuming that the odds were that he would one day be arrested. But on the day that France was liberated he was on the barricades in Paris.

He ran his bureau with the precision of a lawyer and the efficiency of a businessman. Working for him were another ex-officer and an ex-sergeant. The latter was always at his desk. He was as brave but not as lucky as d'Autrevaux. One day about two years after I was captured I was confronted with him by the prison authorities.

'They know everything about me,' he said. 'Don't worry.'

So we embraced, they led him away and I have never heard of him since.

In order to give me a suitable reason for being in Paris I was instructed to resume my studies and work with a definite objective in view which would stand up to investigation if anybody became suspicious. I decided to work for a diploma which was regarded as a qualification for the higher civil service.

Meanwhile my job for d'Autrevaux chiefly consisted of collecting, sifting and organising information which dealt mainly with installations and fortifications all over France. We distributed it to agents who would take it to Vichy. But we also had to be prepared to take it to Vichy ourselves. One of my first assignments therefore—for this Paris office had only just been set up—was to organise a number of places along the line between occupied and unoccupied France where we could cross undetected from one territory to the other. Over a few weeks I made contact with various friendly people, mostly farmers, along the border in the region of Nevers, where we could hide and rest if necessary or through whose woods and fields we could pass without interference. We built up quite an organisation in Nevers. For instance —and we were very proud of this—we contacted a sympathiser in the office of the Prefect, the Governor of the Province, who put us in touch with the driver of the Governor's car. This was a great boon. Often we got papers and maps across the border in the Governor's own car, sometimes when the Governor himself was aboard. Once, I remember, my father, a Czechoslovakian-born German deserting from the Nazis, a colleague of mine from Paris and I all sat quietly in the car, with masses of papers under the front seat, while the frontier police, after a perfunctory glance at the Prefect's car, saluted smartly and motioned us on.

We had various different ways of communicating with the other side of the demarcation line. In this part the river, which constituted the line for several miles, was too broad to swim or row across without being seen. We often used a bow and arrow, tying the papers to the arrow and shooting them over. In the summer if we wanted to get somebody across we would go to a part of the river where the water was shallow and bathing facilities existed on either bank. We would see to it that there were groups swimming on both sides of the river before our man swam out into the middle. The guards would never notice from which side he came in and which side he got out. As time went on we had to pass escaping British airmen across the line and it became necessary to pay local people to take risks. So we had to build up a network of those who would only take risks for money as well as of those who could be counted on to do it out of patriotism.

It was not really my job to help escaping prisoners, but as things turned out—on the side as it were—I must have passed two or three dozen times across the demarcation line. I first became involved through a relative, who told me of a woman in Normandy who had been hiding some British soldiers for nearly six months. She was getting more and more apprehensive about what would happen if she could not dispose of them. And there was I, a naïve, over-confident young man of twenty-six, being asked to arrange to get eight British soldiers out of Normandy and back home, and saying I would see what I could do!

Madame Bouchet de Fareins lived in a big house off the main Honfleur-Deauville road. Five or six German officers and the local Gestapo chief were billeted on her, so it was not surprising that she had become rather apprehensive! The British, one officer and seven other ranks, were scattered around in local farms. Richard Broad, the officer, was living in the home of a remarkable elderly lady who bred mastiffs. He was quite safe here because the Germans were not only terrified of the mastiffs, but they were also rather afraid of Mademoiselle Turgis herself.

It was arranged that Richard Broad should come to see me at Madame Bouchet de Fareins' house, and that night, when everyone, including the German officers, was in bed, he came through the fields, climbed the ladder that was placed against the wall and came in through the window. We had a good talk, but he could not be precise about one thing that it was important for me to know—the physical health of his friends. So the next day, led by our hostess's daughter, Claire, a child of about eight, I went from farm to farm meeting the fugitives. Children make wonderful spies. They are fearless and nobody notices either them or the adults who are with them. I found that although the men were in good heart after several months of confinement, their health was poor. This meant that the journey would have to be made in stages and that they would certainly have to rest for a few days in Paris.

With two other guides besides myself, we set off in the small hours of a very dark night. It was a long walk to the station, right through Honfleur and past the German police headquarters. When we got on to the train we distributed ourselves through three adjoining compartments and buried our heads in newspapers. The four-hour journey went without a hitch.

I had planned to hide the men for a couple of nights at the flat of an uncle who had recently died. I thought I might have some difficulty with the concierge, but again things could not in fact have gone better.

Suddenly the next morning, while we were discussing our next move, the door opened and in came my uncle's daughter-in-law. Her visit to the flat was quite accidental; she had merely come to collect some of my uncle's belongings. As soon as she understood the position she became alarmed. I told her all she had to do was to leave quickly and nobody would be any the wiser. But she insisted that we leave. When I pleaded with her she became hysterical, burst into tears, said I was a lunatic and the whole family would be shot in consequence of my folly. It was a moment of panic and the only thing to do was to leave at once. This we did and within an hour or two I had split up the group, lodging them where I could with friends.

The next day at the main-line station there was an alarming moment when several lorry-loads of Germans arrived. There was nothing we could do at this stage. We boarded the train, distributed ourselves among three compartments again and hoped for the best. Luck was with us. We were squeezed together like sardines and once or twice people got into conversation with us, but immediately the Frenchmen would take over. Whenever possible the other feigned sleep. At Nevers we walked quickly from the station to a small, rather seedy little hotel run by a couple, rough and ready, and rarely quite sober, but always willing to risk their lives for France. We sat down in the small private dining-room. We were in the middle of our meal and more or less off guard, when the door opened and there stood a German policeman. I got up and politely asked if we could help him. He said he was looking for the landlord and had come to the wrong door. Obviously he suspected nothing, so we chatted a little and in a moment or two he wandered happily off.

Soon after midnight we left the town and made for a spot about a hundred and fifty yards from the demarcation line. There stood a remote cottage, set well back in the trees. My British charges were tense. A few hundred yards now and they would be over the first great hurdle between them and their freedom. I went forward. If a certain window was open we must remain where we were until either the window was shut or a colleague came from the cottage and joined us. But if the window was shut it meant that the German security patrol had passed. The window *was* shut. We ran across the meadows and I was able to hand over my charges to friends on the other side of the line.

During the next months I made this journey many times again.

There must have been somewhere around thirty or forty trips I suppose and things went badly wrong only twice.

This was an exhilarating time for me. How I did what I did in physical terms amazes me enough when I look back on it, but that I barely noticed the strain is more amazing still. To and fro to the frontier alone meant averaging ten miles an hour on a bicycle over a period of about a day and a half. It was never safe to hang about; I always returned to Paris the next day.

We were by now being encouraged by our knowledge of the existence of the Free French headquarters in Britain and by the avowed intention of General de Gaulle to continue the struggle and of Churchill to back him up. We had the feeling that we were part of an army. It did not lessen the risks but it made the prospect of victory more real.

One day Simoneau said to me casually:

'I think I might put you in touch with somebody who is working for another friendly organisation. You will be the only person from your Paris set-up to be in contact with it. And your contact will be through just one person. Give any information you feel may be of help, or that they ask for, even if you are giving it to us as well. And anything you get from them you can give to us. That is understood.'

This is how I met the woman known as La Chatte. I went to a restaurant in Paris and soon she came up and got into conversation with me. In the course of her talk she produced a certain phrase. She confirmed what Simoneau had said. After that we met several times and exchanged many documents. For several months this was all I knew. But later I discovered that this woman was the second-in-command of a group of Poles who had been cut off in the South of France at the time France fell. Once or twice I met their chief, a Polish captain. Their organisation was doing many of the things we were doing, but we were told nothing of this. La Chatte had a radio in Paris and was in direct contact with London. It may have been the very first radio link.

Even though we were conscious of its value, our work of compiling statistics and so on was very tedious and we continually wished for more action. I remember feeling this strongly several times while watching the daily parade of German troops on the Champs Elysées, when my feelings of hatred and resentment rose to bursting point. One day I remember putting a hand grenade in my pocket with the idea of throwing it at them; but of course when my hand was on the pin I saw how childish I was being. After that I used the daily parade for 'morale' purposes. Whenever I felt depressed I would go to the Champs Elysées and watch the enemy march past. It made me want to get back to work again and do what I could to get rid of them.

On 21 June 1941, nine months after I had begun my career in the underground, Germany declared war on Russia. The weather in Paris was glorious; the mornings were brilliantly sunny, the evenings soft, warm and delicious beneath the trees of the Bois de Boulogne. But the atmosphere was extremely tense. The French were stimulated and excited; the Germans were apprehensive and on edge—a reversal of the mood of the previous months. We of the underground were naturally enormously encouraged to hear the news that Russia was in; but we knew that we must now take even greater care than we had before.

At that time I lived near the Porte d'Orléans, a quarter occupied for the most part by small bourgeois shopkeepers and office workers. In the middle of the night of the 21st I was woken by the noise of grinding brakes. German police cars had stopped in the street. My first thought was that they had come for me, but there was no sound in the house and the voices came from across the road. Watching from behind the blinds, I saw lights going on in the fifth floor of the house opposite. In a few minutes police stumped down the stairs, a man and woman among them, pulling on clothes, hair dishevelled. The car doors closed on them and the cavalcade drove off. The street was quiet again. I went back to sleep for a few hours before the morning. This scene, however, started me thinking. I decided that for some time now I had been taking too many risks, setting myself too exacting a pace, and neglecting precautions. I decided to change my identity, and generally to go more carefully.

Not long before, I had met an Austrian civilian, Felix, a handsome, gay attractive man in his middle thirties. He spoke no French but quite good English. We talked of England with sympathy, even affection. He had been introduced to me by a young French woman whom I had met through close friends of mine, and who indeed was a friend of mine. She had learned what kind of life I was living and she had done some work for me in which she had displayed intelligence and courage. She spoke very well of Felix, obviously liked him very much and appeared to trust him. She told me that he held a high position in the Siemens works, in virtue of which he received technical reports on the German army. She was convinced that these would be of great interest to us and could be obtained from him.

I was in two minds about Felix. Obviously if all that we had been told about him was true he could be a most valuable source of information, and it was part of my job to recruit informants. But he was, after all, a national from another country and consequently not so easy to check up on as a resident Frenchman. I decided that in any event I would meet him again with the young woman and sound him about the possibility of his being able to help me. Something happened on this occasion which far from diminishing my doubts had the double effect of both augmenting them and making it necessary for me to go on and resolve them one way or another. The girl introduced me to Felix by my real name. Whether she did that by mistake or because she trusted him so much was not clear to me at the time, but as a result of this gaffe I decided first to change my name and address for the second time in a matter of days, and then to try and find out once and for all if Felix was really a suitable recruit.

I met him again several times. He was clearly a very resourceful, well informed and high-powered man. It was not a question of whether Felix would or would not help us but of whether he would help us or turn out to be in league with the Gestapo.

18

It was essential to put him to a crucial test. I telephoned him and asked if I could call and see him at his office, telling him that I wished to bring along some interesting documents about my organisation. My plan was to turn up with some carefully expurgated papers in my document bag. If I were arrested with them on my person I would hope to come to very little harm, but Felix would then be exposed as an enemy. On the other hand, if nothing happened to me, his *bona fides* would be established.

The Siemens block of offices seemed full of Germans. There were a few French people there, but the majority of those visible in the corridors and ante-rooms were German soldiers and German civilians who might equally well have been industrialists or plain clothes policemen. After waiting for what seemed to me a suspiciously long time I was taken up to Felix's office. He was smiling, gay and genial as usual, very much at his ease. I took a chair, a cigarette, and we began to talk in fairly general terms. After a few minutes a bell rang. Felix behaved as though he had expected this signal, asked me to excuse him and left the room. This, I thought, is the moment chosen for the entry of the police. In a few moments the door opened again, but to admit only Felix, still apologising with his delightful charm for having left me alone. After a short talk I left.

The test seemed to have yielded a positive and desirable result. All the same, when I left him I chose a very complicated route back to my lodgings in order to throw off anyone who might try to tail me. I had the impression once or twice that I was being followed.

From this time I was committed to collaborating with Felix. I provided him with an excellent camera and he made careful preparations which would enable him fairly soon to give us copies of certain photographs and documents which we had listed for him. Everything was going well.

On the evening of 9 July, I met Felix with the young woman who had introduced us in a little bar in the Rue Royale. The purpose of the meeting was for him to hand me documents which if discovered by the Germans would have completely incriminated him. When I had arranged the meeting with Felix a few days previously I had mentioned that I would be leaving Paris the day after our meeting for a short stay in unoccupied France. Anybody who knew what work I was doing could have immediately deduced that on the evening in question I would have a great many important papers on me. The package consisted of about fifty typed pages. I also carried photographs and drawings.

Over a drink or two at the bar in the Rue Royale Felix handed me his envelope. Having made all the arrangements for my departure and having nothing urgent to do, I accepted the invitation of Felix and our charming mutual friend to dine with them. I should have preferred to eat somewhere in the centre of Paris, so that I might easily get back to my lodgings in the Place d'Orléans. But one of them—I cannot remember which—suggested a place in the Bois de Boulogne. I demurred a little, pointing out that this would make it difficult for me. However, it was a glorious evening and dinner in the Bois de Boulogne was an attractive prospect.

And it was a very good dinner. The band played Viennese waltzes. It was the last and memorable evening of the civilised life which broke off that night.

After dinner when we made our way towards the nearest Métro station I should have suspected something when they said that they too would take the Métro, for I knew they could have walked home quite easily.

We said goodbye at the bottom of the Métro steps. I went in the Etoile direction, they towards Pont de Neuilly. Ten yards along the dimly-lit tunnel there was a sharp turning. As soon as I had walked round it I found myself face to face with two men in black suits, wearing soft hats and with revolvers in their hands. One of them stepped behind me and pressed the muzzle of his gun into my back. The other, with his gun pointed at me, went through my pockets with his free hand to make sure that I was unarmed. In bad French and in a low tone that I shall never forget, he said: 'Shut up! It's all over!'

Although I had often visualised just such a situation as this, everything happened much more quickly than I had bargained for. I had supposed that there would be at any rate a second or two to try to save myself.

I simply stood there, in front of the revolvers, motionless and dumb. To my shame my first reaction was an uncontrollable trembling and a feeling of having no muscles in my legs. My brain, however, went on working. My first thought was not to make any movement or noise which might endanger Felix. I must not look back to see what had happened to them, nor must I shout a warning to them. I must behave as if I were on my own. Only seconds later I was telling myself that I was an idiot and that it was almost certainly Felix who had deliberately led me into this trap.

My next thought—how swiftly thoughts succeeded each other and how long it takes to describe them—was of what I had on me. There was a little notebook which particularly worried me. I had also, which was worse, a thin piece of paper on which, because I have a bad memory, I had written names and addresses and information which would be useful to me on the journey that I was about to make. I had put this paper in my trousers pocket, so as to be able to get at it easily in case of danger. I saw at once there was nothing to be done about the main package of documents, for I was carrying them in a file I had in my hand. And the notebook was in the inside breast pocket of my jacket and difficult to get at. All I could try and dispose of in the tiny amount of time that I managed to create for the purpose was my list of addresses. It was by far the most important of the papers, since if it fell into the hands of the Gestapo it would have meant the immediate arrest of many of my colleagues.

The policemen were now hustling me towards the street. I was relieved to find that once I started to walk the strength began to flow back to my limbs. The corridors of the Métro were deserted at this late hour, so I saw no hope but to move off between the two men, each of whom held me by the wrist. I have been back to look at that corridor since. It is very short, a mere ten yards or so. But that night it seemed interminable. As we climbed the stairs to the street I was tempted for a moment to try and free myself and dash back down into the corridors of the

Métro. Looking back on it, I regret that I did not do so. I believe that I might have escaped.

We reached the top of the stairs and stepped out on to the pavement. Two cars were drawn up waiting for us about thirty yards away. The night was bright with stars. I went on walking between my two captors. Then, as though giving an order, I told myself that I must at least try to get rid of that list of names.

With a violent jerk I freed one arm and then hurled myself on the other policeman. In a very short and confused struggle, I managed to tear myself out of my jacket. I got away, leaving the remnants in their hands. I hurled my document bag as far away as I could. I don't suppose that ever in my life have I run so quickly. As soon as I was a few yards away I snatched the piece of paper from my pocket. What I did with it I have no recollection. I dare say I crumpled it into a tiny ball and threw it away. It was, as I said, very thin, and in the time it would have taken me to cover a yard or two, I could have got rid of it easily.

I had never thought for a moment that I could escape. I was too good a target. If the guns didn't do their work, there were the cars which on the vast Place Maillot would easily catch up with me. My suit was of a light pale-coloured material suitable for a hot July day in Paris, and my shirt, now exposed by the absence of my jacket, was pure white. I don't suppose I had covered ten yards before the first bullet hit me, just inside my ribs, grazing the left lung. The second hit my foot, although this didn't stop me running, and what I then thought was the third and last bullet hit my leg slightly above the knee and broke it. This was the shot that brought me down. A fourth bullet, which I neither heard nor felt, hit me in the back. There was no pain. I felt nothing. I remember only the sudden impression that the ground had moved from beneath me and the feeling of being mown down.

3

When I regained consciousness, perhaps half or three-quarters of a minute later, I was in a car. The police had thrown me into it like a sack. My first sensation was a feeling of coolness against my cheek, which was forced against the window of the car. Other people had arrived on the scene, presumably at the noise of the shooting. There were a city policeman, a Frenchman with a bicycle, and a woman whose face I could not see. They were received coldly and they seemed to size up the situation pretty quickly. The policeman stammered that he had only come to lend a hand and the woman said nothing. One of the Germans told her in bad French that if she breathed a word of what she had seen, she would suffer reprisals. Then the car began to move and I lost consciousness again.

I recovered consciousness half-way between the Porte Maillot and the Etoile. For the first time I felt pain, a slight ache in my left leg. My hand was imprisoned against my leg and, as it was sticky, I knew I was bleeding. I realised that my leg must be broken because it stuck out at right-angles to the line of my body. I was on the floor of the car, lying where I had been thrown. The Germans were talking to each other. Not understanding German, I caught only the word 'Val de Grâce', 'Pitié' which were the names of hospitals. My brain continued clear for a moment and I remember thinking that we were now passing within a hundred yards of the houses of friends who were doing the same work as I was. I caught a glimpse of the dark mass of the Arc de Triomphe and against lost consciousness.

The next time I came to I was stretched on a table with bright projectors shining in my eyes. Later I realised it was German Police Headquarters in the Rue des Saussaies. A man stood at my side, outside the circle of light. There were other men behind me but I could not see any of them. I was told that I was to be interrogated. I heard the questions that were put to me:

'What is the name of your chief?' 'Where were you going?' 'Where do you live?'

I remember gasping and shivering and at the same time feeling profoundly relieved to realise that I was far too weak to reply and that they must realise this too. My predicament gave me an advantage over them and we all knew it. Indeed, one of them, exasperated no doubt to find that I seemed incapable of answering, shook me by the shoulders. The only result was that I fainted again.

I have no idea how long this initial interrogation lasted. All I know is that I answered none of their questions. I remember a few seconds more of consciousness in the courtyard, as two soldiers carried me to an ambulance. I can still hear the scraping of their boots on the stones.

I awoke the next morning I believe, or the day after, to find myself in bed. Since my spectacles had been removed and I was practically blind without them, it took me some time to realise where I was. All I could make out was that I was in a room, which seemed rather small, that my wristwatch and rosary were missing, and that my damaged left leg was encased in a framework of some kind or other. Gradually I saw that the room was painted white, was clean, had no bars on the window, and I assumed I was in some kind of hospital. I felt very weak and found I could not concentrate. It was very hot and I knew I was streaming with sweat. Even the weight of the sheets was unbearable. Soon after waking I again fell into a heavy sleep. There was a radio playing and I realised later that in the depths of sleep I had heard faraway waltzes making a strange pattern among the dreams which formed and reformed in my head. My memories of that first day are scanty and confused.

The second night I slept much better and I awoke in the

morning calm and rested. As my eyes opened they fell on a German orderly, sitting in a rocking-chair, reading. Mine was the only bed in the room. By its side was a table, but I could not see my rosary, spectacles or pocket-book on it. Behind me was a window.

I had hardly begun to look about me when a nurse came into the room. She was about forty with a face like a dried-up olive. But she had gentle eyes. I assumed she was a German and she was. She looked at me, turned and said a few words to my guard, and my bed was wheeled out into the passage and thence into another room. This was bigger. There was another bed here on which a man lay, wearing only his underpants. A radio played from a corner. The nurse rearranged my pillows so as to lift my head higher and left the room.

The other man, a German, went on smoking and reading a magazine. He appeared to be paying no attention to me. A little later in the day, I felt my right leg gradually slipping, little by little, off the bed, a process which produced agonising pain in my back. The other man heard me moan, saw what was happening, got up, and replaced my leg on the bed, all without saying a word. This happened a good many times during the following three or four days.

At about eleven o'clock that day I received my first visitor from the outside world, a big man with a heavy, florid face, gold spectacles on his nose and a cigar in his mouth. He was a German. He wore a grey mackintosh, held a soft hat in one hand and a heavy document bag in the other. He stood at the side of my bed, asked my room-mate a few questions and then took from his pockets my watch, my spectacles and a bunch of keys. He did not return my rosary. Holding up the keys for me to see, he said in not very good French:

'Are these your keys?'

My first thought was that there was no point in attempting to deny it. They had been found on me and in any case most of the keys would be unimportant. Then I realised that among them was the key of my flat, where there were important documents and firearms. When he repeated his question I answered, trying to sound as weak and vague as possible, which was not very difficult. I said I thought they were the keys of one of the cupboards in my flat.

'But where do you live?' he demanded.

I shook my head weakly, pretending not to understand. His reaction was not as convenient as the others' had been. He came nearer to me and, pushing his red, angry face close to mine, shouted:

'We know your address. Confess. You are only making your case worse.'

I groaned but said nothing. My leg began to slide again. There was no need for acting now, for it was really painful. I moaned and the sweat began to start from my forehead and run down my face.

My interrogator shrugged and turned away, muttering words which I could not make out. I heard him putting one or two brief questions to my room-mate, who apparently acted as a kind of warder, then he came back to my bedside. I asked him if he could return my rosary, which would have been in the pocket of my trousers.

'You won't tell us your address, M. d'Harcourt?' he said, shrugging his shoulders again. 'Think about it. I shall come back. And don't forget, we know how to make you talk!'

I was now exhausted with pain and fright and closed my eyes. I heard him go to the door, saying something to the warder as he left. Now, for the first time, I gave way to a despair which was more a deep sense of loneliness and hopelessness than a fear or anxiety. The papers which my visitor had taken out of the document bag and brandished at me were those I had been carrying two days ago. But it was not the thought that I would almost certainly be shot as a spy that plunged me into this peculiar desperate childish anguish. First, I imagined that I had cut myself off from my comrades by allowing my document file to be captured (although these papers merely contained information about the German army, I did not know at this time that the slip with names and addresses had never been found by my captors). Secondly, I had now subjected my parents to an intolerable burden of grief and anxiety. My mother could not be prevented from knowing what had happened to me, and I could imagine her distraction. I tried to comfort myself with the thought that it would soon be over for her. My guilt would need no proving, my case would not drag on, and the sentence could be confidently predicted. I turned my face to the wall and there, hidden by the sheet which I had pulled over my face, I wept uncontrollably as only a small child weeps.

My warder had left the room just after the Gestapo man. The nurse with the face like a dried olive had come in and was now moving quietly around the room, tidying and dusting. As the tears coursed down my cheeks I sensed her close to my bed. She may have understood how I felt, for she pulled back the sheet to uncover my face. To conceal the fact that I was weeping I tried to turn farther to the wall, but in doing so my leg began to slip down again, and the unbearable pain this produced in my back made me groan. I could not hide my face and I was too weak to go on trying. She took my hand in hers and murmured words which I did not understand but which I knew to be full of sympathy.

She was methodical, quiet and gentle. She lifted my leg back on to the bed. Then she went to fetch a bowl of hot water and washed my foot, which was covered in a filthy mixture of dried blood and muck which made me feel ashamed. Then she dried my eyes with her handkerchief and sat down on my bed, holding my hand in hers. We were neither friends nor enemies; something more universal united us. She gave me my spectacles, which I could not reach on the bedside table, and put my watch on my wrist. When she saw that I was calmer, she left the room and came back with a tray of food. I was not hungry, but to please her I made an effort to eat some of it. Then I went to sleep.

I dreamed, but unlike the dreams of the first two nights, the dream was calm. I was back in my grandparents' home, Grosbois, the old house in Burgundy; and I was among the fawn bindings of the books in the library, with the smell of polish from the parquet floors, and the familiar furniture. All this dusty past came to life and took possession of me.

I awoke calm. Slowly my mind brought me back to my bed in the hospital. Stretched out on the next bed was my warder, reading. When he got up and began to dress, I recognised the uniform as that of a corporal of the German army. His new, shining boots were hard to pull on. Then came one of those unexpected moments of grace and charity. He came over to my bed and asked in clumsy French whether I was a Roman Catholic. When I nodded he took from his pocket a rosary of black beads, a dozen of which were missing. He laid it on my bed and, as he turned to leave the room, he waved his hand.

The rosary had a considerable effect upon me. Until then I had hardly thought of God or of asking His help. That morning during my session with the Gestapo man I had asked to be allowed to see a priest, but I had done so without much religious concern, merely out of a conventional reaction to my belief that my death was only an hour or two away. I had been cheered when he had said that I was in no immediate danger of death. Now, with the rosary, and even more because of the way it had reached me, my heart lifted a little and in the movement my mind turned to the feeling of God. Lonely, forsaken and broken, I looked on the little cross as the symbol of hope, or reintegration, of the way back to parents, friends, colleagues, and the normal lasting life of which this state of pain and doubt and fear was merely an interruption. I held the cross and prayed, and in the next few lonely hours was comforted more, looking back on them, than I would have thought possible.

Often before then, and sometimes now, twenty-five years later, my religion, with its emphasis on sin and the catastrophe of death and the prospect of judgement in another world, has weighed on me and sapped my vitality. But that early evening in that tiny bedroom it lifted my soul from where it had lain exhausted. My parents had always been religious, but they never tried to impose their faith on their children. As a young man religion meant little to me. Now in my fifties I believe God is there, but I do not often go to church, nor do I wish to go. But I was glad to turn to God in my despair. And I am glad to feel that when in my old age I need His comfort, I know from first hand the way towards it.

The next morning my wounds were dressed for the first time. The first time, at any rate, which I remember. About nine o'clock a trolley carrying gauze, bandages, scissors and shining dishes was pushed in by an orderly whom I had not seen before. After him came my nurse accompanied by a German military doctor, wearing a long white hospital coat behind which I could see his shining boots. This was the occasion on which I discovered that I had received a fourth bullet in my back, and realised where the strange and almost intolerable pain had been coming from. An enormous dressing was wrapped round the trunk of my body, underneath the hospital shirt.

The orderly leaned over me and signed to me to put my arm behind his head, which I did. I heard the doctor swearing under his breath. The bandage was soaked with blood and there was a large stain, becoming paler at the edges, on the draw-sheet. They changed it as well as my dressings. The doctor had a thin, dry face, not without breeding. He was never rough and he did what he had to do quickly, efficiently and skilfully. He displayed no emotion. It was his duty to get me out of danger. He spoke to me only once, and that was much later on. I remember studying the exact and elegant movements of his fine hands. After the re-dressing, which did not take long, the trolley was wheeled out. The doctor washed his hands at a basin in the corner and left the room. I was alone again.

They had left the door of my room open. Some minutes later I heard a faint noise and as it became more pronounced I realised that someone was sweeping in the corridor. A woman appeared just outside the door. She looked across at me curiously for a moment, but then went on with her sweeping, continuing her work down the length of the corridor. A few seconds later, probably having assured herself that no one was in sight, she retraced her steps and again stopped by my door. This time, after looking up and down, she came quickly up to my bed, her fingers on her lips. She bent over me and said hurriedly in a low voice:

'I am French and I work here. Have you a message you'd like me to deliver?'

There are times when one must trust to one's intuition, and I had a feeling that I could trust this woman. I whispered the address of one of my aunts, simply asking her to send a message there if she could, to say that I had been caught and to give the name of the hospital where I was. At that time I did not know that I was at La Pitié. She said she would do it and went out at once.

She was as good as her word. Four years later, when I was repatriated from Germany, I found among my things at my parents' home a short anonymous note telling my parents of my arrest and describing the condition I was in at the hospital. I never knew the name of that woman, who without being asked risked her liberty to do me a good turn. I wish I could find her in order to thank her.

For a day or two I began to feel much better. I now had an appetite and I looked forward to the delicious sandwiches my nurse made for me. The hospital food was not bad, but it never varied. Bread and coffee for breakfast, sometimes with a little jam. For lunch a bowl of soup, a plate of salad and a tasteless meat ball, followed by an equally tasteless fruit jelly. The evening meal, which was served at about five o'clock in the evening, consisted of bread and a generous helping of sausage. Evidently I was considered a valuable prisoner.

My fortune seemed to take a turn for the worse when my gentle-eyed nurse was replaced by an extraordinarily strongly-built girl with an enormous bosom. It was clear, as she moved me this way and that to make my bed, or lifted me higher on my pillow, that she found me—of average height and weight—a mere featherweight. I have seldom seen a woman so strong. The new girl did her work conscientiously, but there was no more of the almost maternal tenderness of my first nurse, and no more of the delicious little sandwiches.

While I lay there one morning about a week after my arrest, wondering whether the removal of the original nurse had any sinister significance, the door opened and in came what seemed a very large party—the doctor, my nurse and two or three soldier orderlies. I was very disturbed. I assumed they had come to take me out to be shot. They lifted me on to a stretcher, which they placed on a trolley. I was now sufficiently strong physically and morally to make a deliberate decision about how I should behave in my last hour. For the benefit of those who were looking on I decided to display great composure and dignity. Inwardly I began to pray for myself and for all those whom I could bring to mind.

The route we took increased my fears. At the end of the corridor there was a lift which carried us, I should judge, some distance below ground. Once out of the lift shaft we followed a maze of tortuous passages, dimly and sparsely lit. Our journey seemed endless. I remember saying to myself: 'If I am killed in these cellars, my body will never be found.' At this stage it was not so much the idea that I was to die which disturbed me, but the thought that I was to die alone in utter isolation from my friends and disappear into a limitless blackness. An anonymous death!

At some point in the maze of corridors it came home to me that I was not going to be executed, and sure enough within a few moments we entered another lift shaft and rose back to the surface. There the original orderlies left us and a new squad took over. The doctor and the nurse stayed with me. I was wheeled down another corridor into a newly-whitewashed room. The doctor glanced round, seemed satisfied, said a few words to the nurse and the orderlies and they all filed out. This time my door was not left open. It was slammed and a key turned in the lock. A slight noise drew my attention to the door and I saw that a tiny rectangular opening had been cut in it at a height of about five feet. An eye was watching me through it, but as soon as the direction of my gaze showed that I had become aware of being observed it was withdrawn.

The first thing that struck me about my new room was that

there was nothing in it at all apart from the bed. It was a cell rather than a hospital room. The floor was covered with linoleum, the walls were tiled, the frosted-glass window high behind me did not open, and what fresh air came in was supplied by a ventilator, which was worked from outside in the corridor. The first night I did not sleep at all, my nerves still not having recovered from the scare I had had on being removed that morning. Every quarter of an hour a clock struck. Its note was very much like that of the bell which chimed the hours at Pargny, my home village in Champagne. The night was very still, and I could hear distinctly the loud-speaker in the Gare d'Austerlitz not far away.

During those first two days I was still attended by my athletic nurse. She was rough and ready, and, to judge by one or two things I heard her say, very pro-Hitler, but all the same she was a woman, and one must be a prisoner and wounded to know what comfort the presence of a woman brings.

I missed her sorely two days later when she left and three German orderlies took over. The chief of these, a sergeant, was a dedicated Nazi, but though he was obviously unsympathetic he did not in the least ill-use me. His two underlings were more human. Adolf was round like a ball, an idiot of a man, with something porcine about his ugly face. He understood only his orders. Fritz had the appearance and manner of a blackguard. Before the war, as chauffeur to a Berlin businessman, he had travelled and earned a good deal of money. He told me that the war bored him and he saw no need for it. He had been called up three or four years ago, and, the period of enthusiasm having passed, he let me understand, particularly in the mornings when he came to superintend the cleaning, that he was fed up.

'Up to here,' he used to say, touching his gullet.

Patients who were fit enough were expected to sweep out their own cells, but my broken leg excused me. Every morning therefore, a soldier arrived with a fatigue party to do the sweeping. His party was made up of German army soldiers who had been condemned by a military tribunal for various offences and were serving all or part of their sentences in this fashion.

When there were no guards about I was able to talk to them

in their pidgin French, as I knew very little German. I remember two of these prisoners in great detail. They were both Austrians. Their clothing consisted of tattered sack-cloth, old boots and shirts without collars. One of them was tall with a noble, regular-featured face, curling blond hair and an air of distinction. I asked him what he did before the war and he told me he had been working in a business office in Vienna when the Nazis came. One day he was instructed to give me a shave. While he was lathering my chin he spoke to me in an undertone, giving me the latest news of the war. He told me that the Russians were now hitting back hard and that the Germans were losing a great many men.

His colleague was different. He was a small, dark, close-lipped man, with a lock of hair which fell over his forehead. He never spoke. One day I asked him whether he was an Austrian. He stopped his work, straightened his short body and opened his shirt to show me on his chest a tattoo of Christ on the cross.

'*Ja,*' he answered.

Unfortunately I was seldom alone with these two men for long. When the sergeant arrived I always pretended to be asleep.

Days passed in this way. One day it struck me that I might ask for paper and pencil. To my surprise they were given to me, perhaps in the hope that I might write a confession for the Gestapo. I passed whole days in writing, but unfortunately everything that I wrote has been lost.

During the week French workmen were busy doing some redecorating in the corridor outside my cell. I could hear them distinctly through the door. They whistled and hummed and chattered among themselves, talking of rationing, the black market, pay, girls and all the everyday things that made up their lives. To me, from where I lay, they seemed to belong to another world, and to hear them plunged me into the deepest melancholy. They never tried to look into my cell. I don't think it occurred to them and, if it had, I don't think they would ever have had the courage to do so. Perhaps, unknown to me, they were working under surveillance all the time. But I am still convinced that, had they wished to, they could have communicated with me in some way, without risking half as much as the woman who had swept the corridor the week before. For hours at a time I watched and waited for a sign. It never came. They spoke of the cigarette ration, the wine ration, the bread ration, and when they did not talk they whistled like canaries. Again waves of that feeling of utter loneliness, of being rejected, flowed back into my heart and weighed it down.

One night a stretcher was laid down near my door. On it an Englishman was moaning and crying out in a pitiful voice, begging over and over again for someone to stop. It sounded as though he had been badly wounded or tortured. At last there was silence. The next day the only sound from outside where he had lain and raved was of the painters at work again. I felt in them the epitome of France, unaware of life and death, thinking only of the triviality of selfish, everyday life. The memory of those easy-going painters, symbolising the indifference of many of my countrymen, is one of the most depressing which remain with me of that painful time.

4

One afternoon a few days after I had been taken to my new quarters my door was flung open by Fritz, who to judge by his face and devil-may-care air had drunk too much. Stepping aside with a mocking but not ill-natured flourish, he announced:

'*Ein Kamerad!*'

A strange, frail figure was framed in the doorway. He was a man who looked about seventy years old and he wore the usual German hospital shirt, a kind of abbreviated night-shirt which did not hang down low enough to be really decent. In spite of the heat he had a blanket over his shoulders and was shivering.

He tottered over to the bench which ran along the wall near my bed, carrying a half-filled glass of red wine in his hand. He sat down, saying a few words to Fritz in rapid German in a low and decided tone. Fritz hesitated at first, his eyes wavering; then he left the room, closing the door and sliding the spy-hole along until only a small opening was left. This was all rather astonishing, and I still had not recovered when my visitor said in excellent French:

'I am an Austrian and my name is Dorian Hartung. I have lived in France for many years and my wife is French. I remember your father, for I went to see him before the war when he lived at 113 rue de Grenelle. The third floor it was. There was a dark passage which led to the dining-room, and M. d'Harcourt's study was on the left. If I remember rightly there were green velvet hangings.'

I was amazed by his accurate description. Nevertheless, I was suspicious and wondered to what extent I should trust him. He talked on, shivering all the time, with his eyes fixed on a point somewhere above my bed as though he were lost in some deep private dream. He was like a ghost. His conversation would continue coherently for several sentences at a time and then come to a stop. After a long period of silence he would begin again, sometimes on some other topic. I hardly knew whether it was his instability or his possible motives that I mistrusted. It was hard to believe that he was only fifty as he said he was.

'I am allowed to receive books,' he said in a low tone. 'Also a little money. I give some to Fritz who is kind to me and buys me newspapers. It was he who told me you were here. These are for you.'

Pulling open his nightshirt, he handed me a recent copy of the *Nouveaux Temps* and two or three cigarettes. He lit one for me and it was marvellous.

'I've brought you some wine that Fritz got for me,' he went on. 'Drink; it will do you good.'

I took the half glass of *gros rouge* and never did wine taste so good.

'I can only come and see you on the days when Fritz is on guard. That's in three days' time. You can send letters to me by him. But be careful. One can't trust the other two. It's not that they are bad, but they are stupid.'

I slept badly that night after Hartung had gone. I kept wondering whether he really had the means of getting me back in touch with the outside world. If so, there were all kinds of possibilities. I tried sending him a message through Fritz the next time he was on duty, and was excited to receive an answer and a cigarette almost at once. He wrote full of hope, and as I waited for my next interview with him I still wondered whether I could trust him. I decided to try to test him. But before I could do so I was subjected to my first ordeal.

One morning about two weeks after I had been arrested I awoke with a distinct sense of feeling physically and mentally refreshed. I had passed my first really good night; my strength was coming back and with it hope. At the age of twenty-six the will to live is so great that even a serious bullet wound like mine seemed little to cope with when one thought of the prospect of liberty that recovery held out.

The medical orderlies came in and attended to my dressings, as they did every other day. The wound in my back still bled a good deal and, although the dressing on it was thick, more often than not it was soaked in blood after forty-eight hours.

Lunch came and went. Then I heard footsteps approaching down the corridor. The first man who entered the room was the doctor. He was followed by the big, florid-faced man who had tried to interrogate me on my first day in hospital. There was also a soldier who carried a typewriter and a second man who looked like another policeman. Immediately I simulated extreme exhaustion. I caused my face and body to sag and tried to look as wretched as possible. The doctor came over to me, sounded my heart and said a few words in German to the other man. I think he said it would be safe to interrogate me for an hour. Then he left the room.

The uniformed soldier sat down in a corner and opened up his typewriter. The second policeman came over to me, offered me a cigarette and asked in perfect French how I felt, whether I was being looked after properly and whether I was getting enough to eat. He then asked me several routine questions to establish my identity. The answers could tell them nothing that they did not know already. I gave them the address of my parents' house, which of course they already knew, but I refused to tell them where they were living now. At this their voices became more menacing. They shouted, brandished their fists and even a gun in my face. But it did no good, for I was still obviously weak. What frightened me at the time, I remember, was the thought of what future interrogations would be like when I was well. Sweat began to pour down my face and, feeling really ill now, I would not or could not talk at all. Fortunately the Germans were now also beginning to tire. After they had left I tried to rest a little, but the smell of their cigarettes hung about the room and there was not a breath of air.

Nevertheless, they had gone and I had not been hurt. I recovered my spirits far more quickly this time. I had summoned up enough courage to ask them if I would have to stay long in hospital before my case came up for trial. They said vaguely that I might be here for one or two months, so I had a respite of a few weeks. Obviously I must exploit my meeting with Dorian Hartung at once if it were to be exploited at all.

I decided to test him by giving him a more or less non-committal message to be taken to one of my aunts. She possessed calm, cool courage and would know the people to get in contact with. If I got an authentic answer, then I could go ahead with confidence. The difficulty was to draft the message so that the meaning would be concealed and would not get anyone into trouble.

My mind raced ahead. If I made real contact with my friends outside and an escape became a reasonable proposition, the main drawback would be my broken leg. The wound in my back would not stop me walking, but my injured leg could; and however well I planned an escape I would certainly have to be able to cover a minimum distance of two or three hundred yards. I decided that I would begin to do graduated exercises every day until the time came when I should be free of my pin and sling.

When these ideas were clear in my mind, I gave Fritz a note for Dorian, saying I would like him to come and see me. I began my exercises without even waiting for a reply. I chose the times when all three warders were off for meals. I could only move my right leg and right arm. At first it was not very easy to do anything at all, and what it was possible to do was painful. But at the end of a few days there was a noticeable difference in my strength.

A major difficulty was presented by the elaborate nature of the apparatus, which had been set up to get my broken leg to mend. It consisted of a steel pin passing through my leg beneath the knee, horizontally, from the left side of my leg to the right, with a sort of stirrup fixed to either end of the pin. The stirrups were attached to a cord which ran over a pulley, and were held in tension by a heavy weight at the other end. All this kept my leg in the proper healing position, and off the bed.

I saw that as I could not cut the stirrups from the pin, when the moment came to free myself and get away I could only do so by cutting the cord itself, and leaving the stirrup and pin attached to my leg. This was not a very promising outlook, but it did not diminish my enthusiasm.

The next day Fritz came to shave me. His face was friendly and smiling. He jabbered a few words in French and looking around with an almost laughably conspiratorial air, gave me Dorian's note. In these moments of great comradeship he used to call me 'Philip'—why I hadn't the faintest idea. I, on the other hand, used to speak to him in terms of great respect and regard. He was very easily flattered. He thought himself quite a Don Juan and used to boast to me in a mixture of French and German of the charms of the Parisian girls.

He was to be on duty that evening and I remember how impatient I was for him to come on guard. Everything went well and Dorian came in and sat on the bench, just as he had done the first time. Again he brought me a newspaper and one or two cigarettes. Then he embarked at great length on a harrowing account of his adventures. If his story had not been so terrible, he would have seemed a comic figure with his legs as thin as wires contrasting grotesquely with his heavy, bloated face and body, and his trembling hands and staring eyes. Once he took his gaze from the wall and produced a worn little photograph of a young woman.

'My wife,' he said. Then after a pause he went on with his narrative.

I interrupted him to urge him to think of the present. We must not let ourselves be beaten, I told him, for to lose hope would in our case mean death. We must at least make some effort to get out of our predicament, and, if he really had contacts with the outside world, we might yet escape. He seemed to respond to this, so I now handed him the note that I had written to my aunt. He promised to have it sent by the amenable Fritz.

The next time Dorian came to see me there was still no news.

But the day after that there was a dramatic development. Fritz brought me a little prayer book and a copy of Pascal. The Pascal was mine! It was one of the books which I had left with my aunt, and inside it there was a short cautious note from her. At last I was back in contact with the outside world.

I waited impatiently for Dorian to come again and when he did I opened the subject as soon as he sat down. What did he think of our chances of escaping? But as he spoke it became clear that his mind could not concentrate for long and he kept wandering away from the subject. Moreover, I could see that he was positively unbalanced in his moments of utter fantasy. However, after several discussions the following plan did emerge. Dorian thought that forty thousand francs and a promise of a job in North Africa or England would buy Fritz. The money could be smuggled to us through the intermediary of the almoner. In exchange Fritz must get us civilian clothes to wear to get through the gates of the hospital. I was confident that once we were outside the hospital gates the Gestapo would never catch us.

Fritz agreed and promised the civilian clothes within a few days. My exercises were producing amazing results and I was full of hope. I was cheered to learn that my parents had given the almoner a document bag with the money sewn into the lining. I sent them extensive information in notes conveyed via Fritz. Even Dorian was beginning to concentrate and was sounding really optimistic.

Then Fritz suddenly disappeared, which was disturbing. Adolf said that he had gone on leave. We should have to wait ten more days until he came back. Then there began a long silence from Dorian Hartung. No visits, no notes. I kept his last letter for a long time. I remember the last sentence in it: 'Courage, dear friend, God is with us!' I am glad to think that his last word to me was of hope, that I restored some hope to his life.

Days went by. Oh, those anxious, airless days. The ritual concert on Sundays; the futile voice of the loud-speaker at the Gare d'Austerlitz; the distant rumble of the Métro; the pitiless clock which mocked the village bell as it chimed the hours.

On one of these days they came to X-ray me. The apparatus

was brought in by the orderlies. Then a woman of about thirty entered. I do not know what her job in the hospital was. It was probably that of interpreter between the French and German staff. She was followed by a doctor and two more orderlies. She said to me sharply:

'You are not allowed to say one word. If you speak the soldiers have orders to shoot you. Do you understand?'

I understood clearly enough when the radiographer came into the room. She was a Frenchwoman, young and pretty, who did her work quickly and well. It will be a long time before I forget her. Not even for a moment did she lift her eyes to mine, but in that very abstention I felt her sympathy. I said nothing, but I never took my eyes off her and I am certain that I received the message which she wished to send me. In spite of the presence of the interpreter, of the doctor and the soldiers (who had brought out their revolvers, presumably to keep us intimidated), an immediate sympathy was established between this girl and me. In the delicacy, gentleness and even tenderness of her hands an extraordinary sweetness was conveyed. At one moment, realising that a movement I had just made hurt me, she said, without looking at me, 'I am so sorry. Did I hurt you?' I could not stop myself answering: 'No. Thank you.' And I hope that in the tone of my voice she recognised my gratitude.

Hearing me speak, the soldiers made a movement. The other woman reminded me tartly that I risked being shot if I spoke. I smiled with contempt. Then the French girl left the room. The soldiers put their revolvers back into the holsters and I was alone. That experience fortified my courage and for a long time I carried with me the picture of her beautiful, delicate face. She was the last Frenchwoman I was to see for a very long time.

Ten days went by. There was still no sign of Fritz, although his leave must be over. I was sure now that something had happened to Dorian and him, which meant that my attempt at escape had failed.

I was right. It was ten o'clock on a sultry night in August. I was awake, listening to the faraway voice of the loud-speaker at the Gare d'Austerlitz. The weather was thundery, hot and heavy, and I had thrown off my sheets because of the heat. The telephone rang in the corridor. In a moment or two I heard hurried footsteps approaching my room. The key was thrust into the lock and the light was switched on. My visitors were Adolf, several members of the hospital guard and some plain clothes Gestapo men. The night guards were in full uniform but Adolf was wearing only the official issue short nightshirt and his boots, which he had not bothered to lace up. I remember noting his ridiculous appearance, but I had also seen that one of the guards was carrying a pair of handcuffs. As they approached my bed they made abusive remarks about me in a sneering, rather than an aggressive, tone. I caught the word '*Franzose*'. For a moment I thought this was some kind of heavy German practical joke. But before I knew what had happened they had handcuffed both my hands to the iron frame of the bed. When they had made sure that I could not move, they left the room with an ironical '*Bonsoir, Monsieur!*' and the sound of their footsteps became fainter down the corridor.

The hour which followed was one of the blackest of my life. How could I get through the night stretched out in this position? If I had let myself go and struggled perhaps I would have driven myself mad by the next morning. It was clear that my plot had been discovered. And as I realised my chance had gone, despair overcame me. For a long time I lay with dry eyes, turning over in my mind every possibility of getting out alive and assessing the chances. Having made every sort of calculation, having peered into all the slightest possibilities, I saw that it was hopeless. At that something gave way inside me. Left utterly alone with the wreck of my plans I did what I should have done before, I turned my face to God and asked for help.

It is difficult to describe exactly what I felt. Beneath everything, beyond everything, I felt myself humiliated and defeated. I had been so confident and now my pride had been laid low. There was only one way of coming to terms with my fate if I was not to sink into an abyss of defeatism from which I knew I could never rise again. I must make the gesture of complete humility by offering to

42

God all that I suffered. I must not only have the courage to accept the suffering He had sent me; I must also thank Him for it, for the opportunity He gave me to find at last His truth and love. I remember the relief of weeping as I realised that this was my salvation. Then the inspiration came to me to kiss the chains which held me prisoner, and with much difficulty I at last managed to do this. I am not a credulous person, but even allowing for the state of mind I was in that night, there can be no doubt in my mind that some great power from outside momentarily entered into me. Once my lips had touched the steel I was freed from the terror which had possessed me. As the handcuffs had brought the terror of death to me, now by kissing my manacles I had turned them from bonds into a key. Many times since, when I have thought of death, I have failed to conceive of it as anything other than the end. But in the blackness of that night my faith gave me light. Peace returned to me and I slept quietly, accepting the death which would bring me life.

The next morning my guards were evidently surprised to find me in a relatively calm state of mind. They took off the handcuffs for a short time. I was given a bowl of coffee, some bread and an apple. I ate with an appetite. At about ten o'clock the surgeon arrived, accompanied by another German doctor, to change the dressing on my back. The surgeon untied the weighted cord, which I suppose was in order to prevent my leg muscles from shortening; then with his shears he cut through the two extremities of the steel pin to free the stirrup; and, using the platform of my bed for leverage, he began to pull out the pin itself.

I must say that I had looked forward to this operation with apprehension; but I think the surgeon suffered more than I did. He had to exert tremendous force to pull out the pin and, when it suddenly came out, he was literally catapulted against the wall behind him. While he was looking at my leg, which had mended well, two policemen came in. One of them was the florid-faced man who had interrogated me before. They collected some papers on which I had made innocuous notes about my first thoughts and experiences in the hospital. The sergeant motioned me to get up from my bed, but the surgeon intervened. As a matter of fact I was quite incapable of walking.

It was clear that I was expected to leave this room, if only temporarily. I decided therefore to take my prayer book with me. I tried to hide it under my shirt, but one of the policemen, noticing what I was doing, seized it from me. To my joy the doctor intervened and it was returned to me. The surgeon then picked me up in his arms and carried me out of the cell.

I now discovered that this had only been a few yards from the main door of the hospital. A black Citroen stood outside. I was helped on to the back seat of the car and a blanket was wrapped round my knees. The two policemen in civilian clothes sat in front. A soldier, armed with a machine-gun, sat beside me on the edge of the seat. The surgeon and the doctor, standing together on the steps and smoking, watched me go. I thought there was pity in the doctor's eyes. In the garden wounded Germans dressed in the regulation striped pyjamas sat on benches. They all looked up with moderate curiosity to see the preparations for my departure. The car started. As we passed through the outer gates of La Pitié hospital all my hopes of escape seemed to vanish.

Our route followed the outer boulevards. Before we reached the Porte d'Orléans we had to stop before a market stall which was on fire. People were crowded round it. For a second, in spite of my leg, I thought of trying to jump from the car. But before the thought could pass fully into my mind, the car was moving fast again, and already it was too late. The policeman who drove us was elegantly dressed in civilian clothes. He smoked an English cigarette, the odour of which floated back to me. The journey was short. We had arrived at an imposing gateway, passed through and came to a halt before a flight of steps. The policemen got out and I was left alone with the soldier. We waited about ten or twelve minutes. I caught sight of a little nun, her head covered in a blue veil, her eyes cast down, trotting across the courtyard. Then the policemen came back, followed by soldiers carrying a stretcher.

They lifted me out of the car and laid me on the stretcher. An iron gate opened and the soldiers carried me down a wide corridor. At one moment we met a group of staff officers, wearing red stripes on their trousers. They saluted smartly. My policemen made the Nazi salute. We went through an iron door, followed another corridor and at last came to a grille on which a notice read: *German Military Prison*. Then this last gate was opened and I saw before me an immense hall lighted only with skylights in the roof. It was something new for me. I had never before seen the inside of a prison.

They laid me on the ground. A great big fellow, at least six foot six tall, and built in proportion to his height, picked me up in his arms, and, followed by the policemen, began to climb the stairs. At the first floor he turned to the left. I could read the numbers on the cells: 190—191. At one moment, on the narrow gangway which joined the stairs to the corridor, in order to get me clear of the banisters, my porter had to lift me high in his arms, and for a moment I was on the outer side of the banister with nothing below me. If I had been quick enough I could have twisted out of his grasp and fallen into the well of the staircase. But I lacked the necessary courage and missed the opportunity.

192—193—194—195—196 . . . we had arrived. My porter entered the cell. There was a bed, a blanket, the sling for my leg. When I was stretched out on the bed, the sling was placed under my leg and the adjustments were made. A moustachioed corporal who was in charge of this floor received me—'*Harkurt—jawohl!*' —and exchanged a few words with the police. They gave him one or two directions. They then turned to me asking if I was hungry. When I said yes, they placed an iron bowl, filled with soup, on a stool near my bed. I was given a spoon. Then they all left the room. Two turns of the key in the lock; a glance through the spy-hole; and I was alone.

The food symbolised the change in my condition. The hospital food had not been bad; this prison food was meagre and barely edible. The soup seemed to be made of gherkins. It was very thin and the nutritional value must have been next to nothing.

My cell was about fourteen feet long by about eight feet wide.

45

The bed was collapsible and could be folded back against the wall. Naturally there were no springs, only metal slats, which had the merit of being solid, but the demerit, from my point of view, of being completely inflexible. A wooden stool, or small bench, which served me as a table, was attached to the wall by a chain. A board, hinged to the wall, could also be used as a table. At the foot of the bed a big metal bucket had been placed for me to use as a combined chamber-pot and bed-pan since I could not walk to the W.C., which was in the corner of the cell, next to the door, with a water tap above it which worked by pressing a brass button.

The thick wooden door of the cell was very strong and could be opened from the outside only. There was a grille set into it, beneath which was a small shelf where my food could be placed when the trolleys came round. Above the grille was an oval opening, which the gaoler could open and shut from the outside. Thick glass over the opening protected his eye from any violence the prisoner might attempt. In the corner opposite the W.C. two boards were fixed to the wall to carry coat hooks. There was a white enamel basin, spoon, and a broom for sweeping. Light came through a frosted glass window.

I had no sooner finished my soup than a key turned in the lock and a soldier came in.

'You are not allowed to keep any personal possessions,' he said. 'Give me your watch. Those are the rules.'

I surrendered my watch, then showed him my missal and asked if I could be allowed to keep it. He took it, turned the pages and gave it back.

'Yes, if you wish to.'

He threw a glance round the room and then left me to myself.

I now realised that I was in the famous, impregnable prison of Fresnes.

5

I knew that it would only be a question of time before I was subjected to a full interrogation. This hung over me like a shadow from the very beginning of my stay in Fresnes. The prospect was the centre of my consciousness, awake and asleep. There was no escaping it, no relief. At the Pitié there had been some distractions. There had been visits from Dorian Hartung, the dressing of my wound every other day, the daily sweeping of my room, the comings and goings, the noises of a busy hospital. Here in the prison of Fresnes it was silent. In the part of the prison which the Germans had taken over most of the prisoners were in solitary confinement and the watch was strict. Police dogs prowled continually around the grounds. Where there was the slightest noise we would hear them rush towards it and start to howl with rage. Any kind of communication between prisoners, let alone with the outside world, was difficult in the extreme.

There were a few crumbs of comfort. The first time my soup came in it was brought by an Englishman. As he placed the bowl on the stool beside me he gave me the 'thumbs up' sign, and said between his teeth: 'O.K.?' I managed a nod. It is amazing how one is encouraged by such a thing.

My physical condition, of course, did not improve things for me. The first time I used the bucket at the end of my bed I fainted. In falling, my face struck the edge of the bucket and I broke some of my front teeth. I don't know how long I lay on the floor before I came to and struggled back to bed.

47

Luckily I still had enough strength to realise that I was temporarily at any rate in grave danger of losing control of my nerves, if not of all my mental powers. At first I found that since nobody was allowed to speak to me, and I to nobody, I was getting into the dangerous habit of talking to myself. I even began to tell stories to myself, as children do. After a while I managed to stop myself doing this, because I knew that the Germans would hope that the solitary confinement might make me break down under questioning. At all costs I had to prevent this happening.

The main and overriding danger to my already shaken mind manifested itself a day or two after my confinement began. I had heard noises in the next-door cell from the beginning, the tapping of a typewriter and the sounds of voices. On the third or fourth day I heard shouting, followed at once by cries of fear or pain. Later I heard weeping. To my horror I realised that the cell next door was the interrogation room. I lay there on my bunk, my ear to the wall, my eye fixed on the spy-hole, and listened with my whole being. The very effort I was making to hear and understand was an appalling ordeal in itself.

Interrogations began at eight a.m. and there was seldom silence before ten at night, except on Sunday which was a day of rest. I realised after a few days that I must stop listening. It was weakening, not strengthening me, for my own coming ordeal. Yet once I heard a sound there was an irresistible urge to listen. I made little balls of bread and pressed them into my ears before the interrogations began. While the bread was still soft and fresh this was not much help, but at the end of a few hours it was quite hard and stopped all outside noises from entering. Later I perfected the system by mixing with the breadcrumbs a small quantity of fluff which stopped the bread crumbling.

I also made a practice of taking up my missal and forcing myself to read the office for each day, reciting it like a monk. I added many unorthodox prayers of my own which were not so much prayers as personal conversations with Christ. For if Christ is God for me, He is also above all the friend who understands all difficulties and all sufferings. It was easy to speak to Him of the sufferings; but it was harder when it came to confessing my human frailties and weakness. Of them, then as now, I found it very difficult to speak with confidence to Him who came to earth to share our human life. I drew great comfort from the trust with which I put my difficulties as well as my suffering in the hands of Him who understands all, who forgives all. Prayer therefore was at this time the core and support of my life and will to live.

Within a few days I had come to hope with all my heart that my own interrogation would come quickly. Waiting was the worst torment of all and would only make me less capable of coping with my interrogators. I turned over in my mind all the problems that might come up, trying to anticipate the questions they would put to me and preparing my answers. The nights tired me more than the days, for I was not meant to go to sleep. When darkness fell the warders began their rounds, passing the door every hour till morning. They tied dusters round their boots, so that one did not hear their padded footsteps until they were in front of the door. Every hour the warder switched on the light in the cell from outside, opened the spy-hole, made sure that all was well, and went away. If I appeared to be asleep, he would switch the light on and off several times to wake me up. Often, if I still seemed undisturbed, he would come in and tear the blanket from my face. Then, satisfied that he had really woken me up, he would go away. Often during the next eight weeks I counted the ten or eleven hours of the night. I dozed off from time to time, but I do not think I slept more than three hours in any night. My only thoughts were of how to keep control of myself, how to fight against the weakening of my will, and to protect myself from moral and physical strain so that I should have the strength to deal with my interrogators.

It was now the end of October and the weather began to be cold. A small hole had been made in my window, probably by my predecessor. If I put my eye to it I could see beyond the outside walls to a cottage, a vegetable garden, a lane and three great quivering poplars, whose leaves were falling fast. I only

49

had a summer jacket, a shirt, a pair of trousers and a thin blanket. I had no shoes or socks.

On the fourth of November there was snow for the first time. It was now eight weeks since I had entered solitary confinement and the cold was further undermining my strength. Soon, I felt, the police would be able to do anything with me. I decided to try to make them interrogate me at once. I went to the grille and told the sergeant in charge that I wished to reveal certain information immediately.

Three days later two police officers came to fetch me from my cell. I could still hardly walk and one of them put his arm under mine and helped me to the interrogation room next to my cell. This was about three times larger than No. 196 and had windows in two of the walls. Outside most of the branches of the trees were now bare, but there were still a few leaves falling. I remember thinking that this was the last time that I should see the leaves fall.

In the middle of the room there was a table with a number of chairs round it. I was motioned to one facing a window, with my back to the door. One of the policemen sat down opposite me, the other sat at the side with his typewriter. Both spoke excellent French.

In planning my campaign I had decided that to rely mainly on telling lies would be useless. I had made up my mind to say nothing which might incriminate those of my comrades who would have no means of taking precautions after my arrest. But I could if necessary give information about some of my superiors because I knew that, once my capture had become known to them, they would have changed addresses, identification papers and so on. I intended to say as little as possible, but I would play the part of someone who was willing to tell the Germans all he knew, but whose memory had suffered through ill health and the dimming of his senses caused by solitary confinement.

The first questions, which were to establish my identity, were almost comically formal. It was as though I was being interviewed for a post in the Civil Service. Then we passed on to my activities in the underground movement. I had anticipated this and gave them a fairly full account. I said as little as possible about my Vichy contacts, but went into great detail about our activities in Paris; for I knew that the organisation would have been dismantled within a few days of my capture several months ago. I did not mention the people who had helped us to cross the frontier because they were local residents who would not be in a position to go to ground. I described certain methods we employed, such as shooting messages across the river, for they would already know all about these. I told my story as slowly as I could, partly to make it sound spontaneous and partly to give them the impression that I was more of a physical wreck than I actually was. So long as I kept talking the two men behaved pleasantly; but if I became too hesitant they would say crossly:

'Come along now. If you can't help us you know what is going to happen.'

Sometimes I contradicted myself and again there would be an outburst of impatience.

'Be careful, I warn you. Yesterday you said you met a man called Alex and now you say his name was Jean. If you aren't telling us the truth, you know, you will suffer for it.'

For several weeks the sessions began early in the morning and went on until dark. Sometimes I saw the point of their endless questions, sometimes I did not. I was not tortured. The torture came when I returned to my cell and went over in my mind what I had said, wondering whether I had made any slips. Almost certainly I gave things away, but I was not aware of it at the time. I would fall asleep exhausted not so much with the interrogation as with my own attempt to work out the implications of what I had said.

Sometimes they would start the questioning by going back to the very first words I had uttered and continue by checking my complete statement. The process would take several hours. Sometimes they would dwell on an apparent contradiction or pause to amplify or fill a gap; sometimes there would be no interruption of any kind. At intervals I would be shown transcripts of what I had said to date, which I would be asked to sign.

I wondered constantly what they were really trying to do. Were there among all these apparently insignificant questions a few that, if answered in a certain sense, would give my interrogators just what they wanted? I had no idea.

Often, of course, the questioning would come very near home.

'Now, d'Harcourt, the letter boxes. Your organisation used an elaborate system of places where information could be lodged to be picked up for transmission. You knew that, of course?'

'Yes, I knew that.'

'Tell us where those which you used were located.'

'I'm afraid I do not know.'

'But you must have known.'

'No. It was not my job to deposit or pick up information. I handed it over and received it from the people I have told you about. I did not use the boxes.'

This was a lie, but a reasonably safe one.

'But two weeks ago you mentioned a letter box you were using.'

'I do not think so,' I said, knowing that they were trying to trick me. 'I think there was a misunderstanding. I assure you I did not personally use any of the letter boxes.'

'Last week, d'Harcourt, you told us about the two chief agents you met from time to time. When did you first meet Raoul?'

'I told you. It was the day I returned to Paris.'

'Tell us again where you met him.'

And so it would go on. They were patient, good-tempered, even polite. One day the interrogator told me that my father had been to the prison and left some money to buy extra food for me. He produced some marvellous brown bread. Later they occasionally brought me cake or fruit, thinking perhaps that it would make me more co-operative and give me more strength for talking to them.

On one extraordinary occasion the interrogator came alone to my cell and stayed for more than an hour. He sat on my bed and started to talk in a long passionate monologue. Why were the

French so hostile to the Germans? We are decent people, he said, as you are. Why must we fight and hate? Why couldn't we understand each other and live in peace? At times his voice rose and I felt that he was on the point of breaking down and sobbing. There in my room he was a very different creature from the efficient officer who put question after question to me in the interrogation room. I was alarmed by his tenseness and wondered if his feelings would explode in some outburst of resentment against me. Looking back on it, I cannot account for his behaviour. Once I thought it was some kind of trick, but by then the interrogations were nearly over. The incident took place just after the fall of Stalingrad. Perhaps he had suddenly had some vision of how things were going to end, and of the futility of it all. I do not know.

My tactics, I discovered years later, were successful. The police took notes of everything I said and concluded I was being fairly co-operative. But not a single one of the principals with whom I had been working was arrested. One or two were taken a year and a half or two years later, but I do not think that this could possibly have been in any way due to anything I might have said about them. The police, apparently, assumed that I was a genuine collaborator, and that in me they had a valuable voluntary source of information. There were two occasions, I remember, when I suddenly bit my tongue in the middle of a prevarication that I felt must have aroused their suspicions. But in both cases they apparently noticed nothing.

Gradually they gave up interrogating me every day. A couple of days would go by without questioning; then the intervals lengthened to a week at a time; then to two or three weeks. When the interrogations finally ceased, I felt a great sense of relief. But soon after that came a severe reaction from the effort I had made. I awoke in the morning with my hands and arms blue with cold, and my brain so numb with nervous exhaustion that I was not fully conscious. Exercise only left me colder. The faster I walked the six paces of my cell, the more quickly I used up the few precious calories provided by the meagre daily ration of soup. I think I must have lived in a state of continuous half-insanity.

I remember turning over in my mind weird childish notions of doing a swop with my gaolers. If I allowed them to cut off a leg perhaps they would let me go free. Once I was on the point of calling the warder to offer an eye in exchange for my liberty. At least the interrogations were over, but they had left me drained of all my resources.

6

As the winter of 1941–42 wore on I felt myself regaining my faculties, and on 5 January something happened which so heartened me that I was completely sane again by the end of the month. It was the day for the barber. But when he came into my cell I saw that this was a new man. He was young and self-confident, with an open, lively face. As he lathered my face he whispered:

'The Americans are in the war!'

This good news combined with the contact with a friendly spirit was exhilarating. Undeterred by the warder who stood at the door while I was being shaved, the new barber asked me in a whisper if I was condemned. I made a negative movement with my head and, talking as quietly as I could between my teeth, said:

'But it won't be long now. I know what I'm in for.'

There was silence for a moment. Then he whispered:

'If you like I can get word passed outside.'

I glanced at his face. Again it was one of those moments when a man must decide within a second whether he will trust or not trust, and commit everything to the decision. I risked it.

'How?'

'Tomorrow, with the coffee.'

I hardly slept that night. The next morning I was on edge from the moment I heard the first breakfast trolleys. My ear followed them every inch of their journey until they reached my floor.

When one of them stopped I was out of bed in an instant, ready to hold out the bowl to be filled at the shutter. The light was switched on from outside by the soldier who followed behind the trolley. When the shutter opened I could see that the man with the trolley was indeed the barber, but he showed no sign of recognition.

'Watch out,' he whispered as he thrust the bowl back through the grille. Then the shutter closed and the light was switched off. I lifted the bowl carefully and felt about on the shelf. Where the basin had been put down there were a few sheets of paper and a tiny pencil. I carried my treasure to the bed and hid it in the mattress. Then, as I waited for the daylight, I drank what seemed to me the best coffee I had ever tasted.

As soon as it was light I read the message.

'I am a French patriot,' it ran. 'I am sending you pencil and paper and will arrange to have your letter delivered by my wife, who comes to see me every week. Give me back the letter and pencil tomorrow at coffee time. But be careful for the watch is very strict. Destroy this note.'

It was not an easy matter to write my letter with my eyes fixed on the door and my ears strained for every sound. Nor was it simple to return the letter and pencil. But what a joy it was to hear the trolley carrying it away down the corridor. It reached my parents in less than a month, thanks to the brave man who risked so much for me.

In its way solitude is an enriching experience, and it was as well that I was able to find it so, for I was to be in solitary confinement for two and a half years. The first effect it is likely to produce on one is an examination of the conscience. Every now and again it is necessary to take stock of oneself, but in normal circumstances few of us give ourselves the time to do so. For many of us in Fresnes this was the first time we had really been alone with ourselves. Millions of industrialists, tradesmen, householders make an exact balance sheet for their activities. The solitude of prison is an excellent climate for establishing one's interior balance sheet and for that internal dialogue which is a necessary function of spiritual life. Indeed there is a real advantage in being brutally detached from nature and the outside world. For the world which surrounds us, and which makes such calls upon us, is a mixed blessing, an obstacle to the life of the spirit, as well as a support. It is not necessarily true that permanent contact with humanity brings us nearer to man. The fact of being alone makes us aware of the problem of our relationship with others. In my case it was necessary for me to be a long time alone to become conscious of my human responsibilities. Solitude develops in one the sense of that responsibility. It was in prison that I came to develop a sense of life as a series of connections with other men, the sense of human solidarity, which is one of the essential components of our life—consciousness in society.

Later, at Buchenwald, I experienced another kind of sense of solidarity, a solidarity that bound men together in a degrading and ultimately destructive way. The awareness of this seemed to kill all that was best in man, the sense of gratitude for being alive, the sense of the gift of one's individuality which is Christian, but also the sense of a value of common humanity which is vital to our life in society.

My solitude at Fresnes gave me the desire, the need to communicate spiritually with all the other lonely people who surrounded me. This seemed to me then, as it does now, to be what solidarity really means. The solitude which men rightly seek to avoid because it is sterile and paralyses is that which consists essentially in the feeling that we are chained in an ineluctable way to other people and cannot escape. To remake true life-giving contact with mankind it is necessary that our being, at its deepest level, should feel the necessity of this intimate, interior link, which is hidden beneath the rubbish of conventions, and of exterior necessities.

In prison I discovered this necessary link, this intimate and profound link, and saw what many have discovered: that it is from there one must start in order to arrive at that love of one's neighbour which Jesus Christ teaches us, and on which is based all morality that merits the name. I saw so clearly in prison how the *conventional* necessities which bind us to each other so often engender only indifference, indeed hatred. With an act of will flowing out of love we can, on the contrary, reach through the solitude of another being and make contact. So long as we do *not* assimilate the pains and the joys of our neighbours, we shall not be able to achieve the profound meaning of the word 'solidarity'. It seemed to me, thinking laboriously through these elementary thoughts, that there will be no true democracy unless it is based on a true solidarity; a solidarity based on love, on a will to understand, on a readiness to be in contact with one another, disengaged from all material contingencies.

In the solitude of Fresnes, therefore, there came an unexpected feeling of enrichment. There was also a sense of pride. One felt that one had been able to dominate the difficulties of the solitary existence and to despise the joys and pleasures of which one had been deprived.

There is, and this must sound paradoxical in view of what I have said about the linking power of solitude, a curious dehumanisation of experience arising from it which allows a man who can rise above it to feel beyond the capacity of his ordinary powers and to think himself superior to ordinary human beings. In solitude man is conscious of a real power, in the detachment—the contempt even—which he can feel for the human state which threatens normally to invade him, and above which he has now managed to rise. This is perhaps a rather Nietzschean idea, but it is only part of the paradox, compensated for by this search of which I have spoken, of a more perfect love for one's neighbour.

These were the kind of thoughts I had as I walked round and round my cell, carrying out my daily programme of physical activity. I used to walk as far as my strength would allow me, at least a thousand times the length of the cell. It was the equivalent of a walk of about four kilometres, enough to keep me fit for any eventuality.

In spite of my strict régime I believe my mind might soon have given way. Fortunately, before it did so I discovered a most important new possibility; a method of communicating with my neighbour in the next room.

The method of tapping on the wall was a simple one. We did not know the morse code, but our system was one tap for A, two taps for B, three taps for C, and so on up to K. From L to Z we preceded each set of taps with a quick double tap. L was tap-tap one tap; M was tap-tap two taps, N tap-tap three taps, and so on. The division of the alphabet into two parts was simply to cut down the number of taps required to spell out the later letters of the alphabet. I tapped with a wooden cross which I had made by carving a piece out of my table with a spoon sharpened on the rim of the lavatory basin.

It was a long time from our first sympathetic taps until the day when my neighbour and I were really able to carry on a conversation. But at length I learned that he was an industrialist from Rouen, that he had a little house in the country on the banks of the Seine, and that his children had been educated at a school where a friend of mine was headmaster. We did even better than this. We were able almost every day to play chess by each marking out our boards in our own cells and tapping out our moves through the wall. My board was marked out on the plank that was my table with a little bodkin I had found in a crack in the floor. I made the men from pieces of coloured paper, bits of metal, stone, straw, glass or wood. Occasionally a warder came in while I was playing and, if he was in a bad mood, he would throw my chessmen on the floor. But more often he would watch me pityingly, probably thinking that I ought to have been in a lunatic asylum rather than a prison.

But my neighbour was taken away one morning, in the middle of a game we had started the evening before. I finished the game alone. He won and since that day I have never played chess again. I do not know what became of him, but I should like to tell him that he won the last game.

When he was gone I would walk, limping up and down my cell, all through the day. There were some marks on the wall which I had previously noticed, but which now suddenly seemed to be a plan and not just the scribblings of a madman. Having thought about it for some time, I had a brilliant idea. On hands and knees I reproduced the drawing on the floor, with the exact measurements of those on the wall. Then I scratched in the dust between two floorboards and found a length of lead, about an inch long, extracted from a propelling pencil. This was a tremendous find and an enormous boost to my morale.

After that I always looked carefully at the inscriptions on the walls of any cells I occupied and, as a result of reading and interpreting, I nearly always found a store of pencil leads or a piece of metal sharpened to a point or edge to make a rough knife. Later, when I was allowed to receive parcels, I in my turn left a little hoard of useful objects and inscribed my plan upon the wall.

The police know what they are about when they condemn a man to solitary confinement. Nothing is more demoralising or more wearing than that anxiety without an end or focusing point. Anxiety and waiting became in the end a real suffering. I think there is no man who would not prefer pain to that kind of suffering. On the few occasions when I had a bad physical pain in prison I almost welcomed it as an alleviation of my suffering. I remember bad attacks of toothache, that continual gnawing pain which completely holds one's attention. One's whole self and consciousness is concentrated on the pain. Perhaps, when a pain is permanent, it becomes a suffering. But the quality of pain is to bind one to the instant, while suffering binds one to time. Pain is a wound, a blow, a toothache. It touches only the periphery of one's being, but suffering penetrates all the defences and takes its seat in one's heart. Against pain man finds himself defenceless, there is nothing he can do but bear it, he submits passively, but meanwhile, in this very passivity, he finds a relief, for pain distracts him from everything which surrounds him, so that he concentrates his entire attention on the part of his body affected by it. Pain is a severe trial of character. With strength of will one can limit it, keep it within the bounds of its own domain. But suffering shrouds the whole of one's being, it is a burden on one's whole self. There is no question of rejecting it. One must analyse it, penetrate it, be penetrated by it. That, it seemed to me, was where the nobility of suffering was to be found. It obliged us to examine ourselves thoroughly.

I remember a day during the winter of 1941–42 when, after an interrogation which had gone badly, they brought me back to my cell and locked me in. I had not been there more than a quarter of an hour, pacing backwards and forwards like a wild beast in its cage, reviewing over and over again the points the interrogators had raised, and anxiously recapitulating the various blunders I might have made, when suddenly the door was opened and two soldiers came towards me. I had not time to notice their rank. They seized me by the collar of my jacket. I was so surprised that for the moment I did not defend myself. In less time than it takes to tell, they had set upon me with their fists and knocked me flying into a corner of the cell. All without a word said. One of them came over to where I lay on the ground and began to hit me again. I lost consciousness, and when I came to, they had gone, and I had nothing to do but see what harm they had done. Four teeth were broken. As I knelt over the W.C. and spat out blood and pieces of tooth, I remember that my first reaction was one of fury. I wondered if they would come in again, and my heart quickened, but the first and immediate effect of the attack was to put me once again in contact with the real world, and this enforced return to reality, though of a disagreeable nature, was an excellent thing.

7

By April 1942 I was only being questioned about once a month, and when towards the end of that month a warder came to fetch me with the usual brusque 'Tribunal, monsieur,' I was not particularly disturbed. I assumed it was to be the usual routine interrogation.

As I went in to the interrogation room a man turned round to face me. I was completely unprepared to see W., the secretary of my organisation. He recognised me instantly, his face lit up in a smile, and he jumped to his feet. We spoke freely, saying all the simple, banal things that one does say at moments of deep feeling. The meeting lasted only a moment or two, for it was soon clear to the Germans that neither of us was going to say anything that could help them. I was soon taken back to my cell. W. was shot some time later.

This was my first experience of a 'confrontation', and it was of great importance to my morale that at the time it was a happy one. My second confrontation, by contrast, was a terrible experience. D. had been a friend of mine since 1940. He was a man of cool courage, balanced and clear-sighted, who seemed to possess the perfect qualities for a secret agent. I had known of him as 'Noel' for some time before I met him and he was an important link in our organisation.

I had calculated, during my long sequence of interrogations in November and December of the previous year, that he was among those whom I could afford to talk about without giving much away. I confidently assumed that he would have changed his name and identification papers within a few hours of my arrest months and months ago. So I had mentioned this Noel who worked with us and who was a specialist on aviation subjects. When they asked me where he lived, I had thought it easier and more cunning not to lie; to say that I was not sure if it was the XVIe or the XVIIe district, but that it was certainly one or the other. This information seemed quite unimportant, otherwise I would not have given it.

A few days after my confrontation with W. I was called to another interrogation. This time I was alone. The questions were on points of detail about our installation in the rue du Ranelagh and did not seem dangerous. I had the feeling of playing an easy wicket, and this was my undoing. The interrogator offered me a cigarette and asked in a casual tone:

'You said, didn't you, that J–L., D. and Le V. belonged to your organisation at that time?'

'That's right. You asked me that ages ago,' I answered, without thinking.

The policeman turned his gaze away and consulted his papers.

'But I thought you told me,' he said, 'that J–L., Noel and Le V. were members of your organisation. Wasn't that it? Evidently then D. and Noel are the same person.'

I hung my head. I had nothing to say. I had fallen into the trap. I went back to my cell with death in my soul, asking myself if D. were already arrested. Such are the secret thoughts of pride and mortification that I even half hoped that he had been, for in that case the slip could hardly matter. But *had* he been arrested? The next few days were agonising.

On a lovely spring day, a week or so later, the policeman came for me again. In the interrogation room a man was again seated with his back to me, and for a moment I thought it was W. once more. But as he turned round towards me I saw that it was D. There was the beginning of a smile on his face as I entered. I could not stop my features easing into a smile too and, as I came towards him, I put out my hand. But as D. rose to his feet, his face hardened and became blank. He looked at me stonily, then turned to the interrogator and said:

'No, I don't know this man.'

My own face must have given a quite different impression. The policeman studied me carefully for a moment, and then said to me:

'Don't you know him?'

'I thought it was Noel,' I stammered, 'but I must have been wrong.'

The policeman smiled sardonically:

'But of course it's Noel—D.—whichever you like! And if you won't admit that you knew him the record of your interrogations is there to prove it!'

With the back of his hand he rapped on a dossier which was lying on the table.

'Would you like me to read out what you said?'

I do not know what I thought I was doing. What followed will always remain a shameful memory. I suppose, on seeing D. there, I considered that the game was up and there was no earthly point in either of us not admitting it. I turned back to him.

'There isn't anything to be done, is there? They've got us. There's no shame in facing it. We've done our duty.'

D.'s face became icy. I trembled. It suddenly struck me that if he, Noel, had decided not to give anything away, it must be because he had more serious reasons than I for not doing so, and that I ought to have realised this instantly and done all I could to back him up. To my shame I had acted as I did more than anything out of terror at the thought of having, in the light of *his* appearance, to go over the whole story yet again. I had got away with a suitable version once, and my heart failed me at the thought of having to run the gauntlet again.

The interrogator was becoming impatient.

'M. d'Harcourt, if you are lying about this, how are we to know you haven't lied about other things too?'

I could not restrain myself.

'Yes,' I said, 'I recognise Noel. I don't know why he pretends not to know me. I have done nothing dishonourable; we have both done our duty.'

At that moment D. turned his face to me. I shall never forget it. He was dressed in blue pyjamas. His feet were bare, and he shivered with cold. I would rather be dead than be looked at again as he looked at me then. He despised me. My sense of guilt so bowed me down that I dared not say goodbye to him. I turned and left the room.

D. never spoke, then or thereafter. Soon after, he died, as he had lived, his spirit unbroken to the last.

For months I was tortured by the memory of his final glance at me. It was worse than any form of suffering I had previously undergone. For months, through sleepless nights, I carried in my mind's eye the image of his face, an ascetic face drawn fine by fatigue, anxiety, and the privations of prison, a face turned towards me with that slight, controlled smile of disdain.

Some degree of calm, of peace of mind, came back to me only when a few months later I was moved into the second division of the prison and by a happy chance came into contact with Legraverend. Legraverend was an industrialist, who had also been sent to Fresnes after being caught in espionage. He was more up to date in his knowledge of the underground than I was, and he assured me that D.'s arrest had nothing to do with me, and that our confrontation could not have aggravated his case. It was only after I had tested him and had satisfied myself he was telling the truth that I regained the will to live. It is curious and indeed encouraging that in conditions where self-preservation is uppermost in a man's mind, he can find his survival threatened most of all by his own sense of shame.

I was now much more in a mood to appreciate the parcels which I was allowed to receive from my parents. What food for the gods that first parcel contained, with its biscuits, sugar and meat. But after two delicious sandwiches, followed by chocolate and sugar, I was sick, more upset than I had ever been in my life. It was the same with the tobacco. Having been without it for fifteen months, my first pipe had a disastrous effect. I had not been so ill since, as a child, I smoked my first cigarette.

During the months of September and October the prison went through a considerable period of reorganisation. Half of the third division, in which I was confined at this time, was now allotted to women prisoners. The second division was emptied of the French criminal prisoners who had occupied it until then, and a number of political prisoners, including me, were transferred to it. I left cell 196 with joy. Living for over a year next door to an interrogation cell had been an extra ordeal; at least I was to be relieved of that. The changeover, which involved many prisoners, was made with an efficiency and cruel thoroughness which was characteristic of the Germans. The whole move took only twenty minutes and was conducted so that I hardly had a glimpse of the faces of any of my fellow prisoners. Had I not experienced it, I would hardly credit it.

My new cell was extremely squalid; 196 had been comfortable by comparison. The floor boards were half rotten, the walls being covered with uninspired repetitive inscriptions—many *Mort aux vaches*, and hammer-and-sickles.

And I had lost my view. The sight of the countryside from 196 had been a great comfort. I had been able to see little vegetable gardens and a farm track and, as the months had passed, I had come to be able to identify nearly all the people who used it. Sometimes on a Sunday I would see strangers wander disconsolately along the track, throwing anxious probing glances towards the expressionless façade of the prison. I presumed that they were parents, trying to guess where a son was lodged. One day in spring I saw a whole family instal themselves in a field nearby. The children were gay and danced on the grass, making their young mother join them in a ring. But from time to time she threw long searching glances towards the prison. Perhaps her husband was there somewhere, watching his children play.

When I moved into my new cell and managed to open the frosted glass window, I was bitterly disappointed to find that all I could see was the interminable skyline of the third division block from which I had just come. This would have depressed me

66

greatly, if I had not discovered that my new cell had very definite advantages.

The prison heating system (which no longer functioned) was conducted through pipes which ran along the top of one of the walls of the cell. In this pipe there was an opening where the vertical pipe from the cell above entered my cell and passed on down to the floor below. It struck me that this opening could well be a means of communication with my neighbours, and this idea cheered me considerably. I was also suffering much less from the cold, as a parcel of splendid woollen clothes had just arrived from my parents.

The parcel arrived in a big suitcase, which the warder dumped on my bunk. Its arrival gave me enormous pleasure, for I felt the presence of my father and mother close to me in the things so lovingly collected. As soon as the warder left me alone with my treasures, I took each thing out and examined it minutely for any messages that might be hidden. I remember the little figs, carefully dried by my uncle, which seemed to bring the sun of the Midi with them into my cell. I was allowed not only to receive a parcel once a month, but also to send dirty linen back in the same suitcase. This opened up possibilities of sending messages to my parents, and I foresaw hours of pleasant distraction.

I soon got into contact with my neighbour on the floor above. One afternoon when the prison was quiet, I was on my hands and knees trying to make the floorboards shine with the handle of my broom, when I thought I heard a voice calling me from close by. I stopped polishing and listened.

'Hullo, hullo, the third floor here. Who is in the cell below?'

I jumped on to the plank which served as a table, so that I could get my mouth close to the opening in the heating pipe.

'Hullo, hullo, this is the second floor. Who is speaking?'

'This is Paul, the third floor. Who are you? What's your name?'

'Hullo, I am Pierre . . .'

But I had no time to finish before I heard a sound at my door.

67

'Look out!' I called, and jumped off the table rapidly. The spyhole in the door of my cell was slowly opening; the warder had obviously heard me. His key turned noisily in the lock.

'Were you talking?' he asked angrily.

I denied it vigorously, but he clearly did not believe me. However, he seemed content to leave it at that for the time being. He grumbled something about talking being forbidden and left the room. As soon as the sound of his footsteps had faded away, I went back to the heating pipe.

'Hullo, Paul. Are you there? I nearly got caught.'

'Be careful,' came Paul's voice through the pipe. 'This is a bad time of day. Call me in the morning at soup time.'

I was jubilant. If the spyhole had been open, the warder would have seen me smiling to myself for the rest of that day. The change of cell certainly was for the better. Also, coincidentally with the arrival of women prisoners, the food improved. We now had half a bowl of soup instead of only a third, and it was much thicker.

I talked a great deal with Paul in the next few days, and soon I felt I knew him well. He was a militant communist. He had gone to Russia twice for the famous May Day celebrations, and he spoke of the far-off U.S.S.R. as of a lost paradise. He was frank, intelligent, and not at all sectarian in his outlook. We had diametrically opposed political backgrounds, but this did not seem to matter in the least. Indeed it made our discussions more exciting.

He had the greatest tact and it was only by chance that I learned that he did not receive parcels. He had been at Fresnes for four or five months and, in spite of the improvement in the food, was already having to tighten his belt. I began to think of a plan to send him something to eat. It was not easy, but it was amazing what could be done. Paul made a rope with his vest. We were both able to open our windows a little way, although the warders fancied they had nailed them fast. I made up a substantial parcel of food and we waited until night came. When Paul tapped twice on the floor above, I opened my window a little way and prepared to tie my package to the string which he would let down. My heart stood still for a moment when I saw the precious parcel swinging in the air at the end of the fragile string. But all went well. After this I always fixed a second string to the parcel, in case his should break. The system worked well; but in the end we abandoned it owing to the risk. We could have been so easily seen from the windows of the third division opposite. It was then that I had the idea of using the vertical section of heating pipe which came down into my room from his. Paul let his string down the pipe; I attached a sock filled with food, and he hoisted it up again. This also worked well.

One day a warder came into my cell just as I was in the middle of the operation. Fortunately he thought I was merely trying to talk through the pipe. He was angry and by way of punishment he took away my mattress, shouting that I would have to go without it for three days. Nor did it end there. The next day two other warders came in and searched my cell from top to bottom. As they were about to leave, it occurred to them to search me as well. They found a pencil. This, they evidently decided, required punishment. They told me to take off all my clothes and stand to attention in the corner of the cell. They then opened the window and the door. The draught was freezing and it was a miracle that I did not catch pneumonia. The sergeant in charge of the floor, a nasty-tempered little man, with a short, brown tooth-brush moustache which had earned him the name of Adolf, was called in to see what they had done to punish me. He seemed satisfied with the humiliating sight I made, but proceeded to collect my books which he then took away with him.

After I had stood there several minutes, and had begun to shiver uncontrollably, a warder came back into my cell, told me to dress again and to follow him. I was taken to the ground floor, into a well-heated and lighted room, where there were an officer and some office orderlies. I stood in a corner of the room, dazzled by the light. The officer was reading a Paris newspaper (I tried—unsuccessfully—to catch a glimpse of the headlines). He lifted his eyes from the paper and said:

'*Harkurt—jawohl*. You are forbidden to talk, Monsieur. Where did that pencil come from?'

I stammered something which he did not catch. But luckily he did not seem to care much whether I answered or not. He probably knew from experience that in prisons there were plenty of stores of pencils in the cracks between the floorboards.

'You will be forbidden to receive parcels for six weeks.'

And he put his nose into his paper again.

It was a catastrophe, not only for me, but for Paul. Without books, extra food, letters or mattress—though this was restored after eight days—I was forced to resume my old life. But it was the old life with a difference, for now I had the companionship of Paul. And now Legraverend, the man who cheered me up about D., was in the cell below me on the ground floor. Very intelligent, with a strong and sympathetic character, he was the best possible friend a man could have in circumstances like those. He also received parcels, and during the period of my punishment he sent me food, part of which in turn I passed to Paul.

The three of us conducted political discussions through the heating pipe. Paul and I, as I have said, disagreed on many fundamental matters, but in Legraverend I found an ally. He was older, wiser and more mature than I was. He was a redoubtable adversary for Paul, particularly on questions of economics. Our discussions were always good-humoured. We recognised one another's faults and errors as well as our own. If I should ever come across Paul again I hope that we would understand one another as well as we did through the pipe at Fresnes, and that we would be as ready and willing to see the merits of each other's point of view and the defects in our own.

The time had now come to try out my project of getting into secret communication with my family by means of my monthly package of soiled linen. My warder's orders were to open and inspect my incoming parcel in my presence, and to go through my dirty linen in front of me before he took it away. How scrupulously he carried out his search depended on what mood he was in. Sometimes he was thorough, as he should have been; at other times he was perfunctory. After having observed him and pondered the matter, I became sure in my mind that even if he or any of his colleagues were efficient on all occasions, I could conceal messages which would get past them.

My first attempt, nearly eighteen months after my arrest, was a failure. I slit the cuff of a shirt, inserted a message on a small notebook page and sewed it up again. Unfortunately it was so well hidden that it was never found. The problem was how to hide messages in places which would be obvious to my parents, but which would not be equally obvious to the guard. And here I had a great stroke of luck. Legraverend was in secret communication with his wife and he took a great risk in letting me in on his system. It was through his generosity and unselfishness that I was able to make contact with my family. I asked my mother, through this system, to open the dried figs that my uncle was in the habit of sending me and to slip an experimental message inside one of them. When the anxiously-awaited figs arrived, the message was there. The plan had worked perfectly.

Now that I had a dependable method of communication, there was a great deal that I could do. I was able to send and receive messages through my family for prisoners who had no means of doing so themselves. For instance I was able to get news of Paul's wife, of whom he had heard nothing since his arrest. I was also able to send a certain amount of secret information—news of recent arrests, etc.—which in turn my parents passed on to my old colleagues in the underground. After the war I learned that this had reached London safely. It was wonderful to feel that even in prison, and even in such a small way, one could help the war effort. Quite apart from being useful, the operation was a great distraction.

I mentioned earlier that we in the second division were imprisoned opposite the building where the women were lodged, and we could look down into the yard where they exercised. When they were out in the yard, hundreds of pairs of eyes watched them through the tiny openings. It was a sad sight from which I often used to turn away to pace up and down my cell. Many of them were so very young. They would stand still for minutes together, their faces turned up towards the blind wall of our building, strained and drawn, searching for some sign of a husband, father or brother.

At that time the discipline of the prison had become a little more relaxed. In the evening, when the women prisoners were not prevented from singing, messages could often be called out.

'René asks for news of Janine.'

'Jacqueline wishes to tell Jean that she is in good spirits and hopes he is too.'

Sometimes a father asked for news of his daughter, or a mother for news of her son. Messages of encouragement often came to us from the women's side. One woman used to risk shouting almost every day: 'Courage, men!' Even in prison they remained maternal to the last, forgetting their own misfortunes in trying to protect and support those who needed it.

Paul, who had broken a pane in his window, was a specialist at sending messages. He had one of those voices that carried. In April 1943 he announced the idea that on the first of May the men and women of the prison should join each other in singing the Internationale and the Marseillaise. The advance arrangements for this performance required some patient planning on both sides. I must say I was not accustomed to singing the Internationale and it contains a number of proposals concerning the first bullets being for the generals, which I, coming from a family of soldiers, could not agree with. But I have never sung with such gusto as on that day when we all sang the Internationale together.

The thought of how the performance had been arranged and what it signified added the power of its emotion to the feeling of the songs. Paul had opened his window so that his voice should carry better. I did the same. A young girl opposite had done even better. She had climbed on to the window ledge of her cell and stood there singing, with her body pressed against the bars. She had a fine voice and I shall never forget how she seemed to pass through the bars and soar towards the sky as she sang.

Of course the performance was not allowed to last very long. Within seconds of the opening notes there was the sound of jack-boots on the stone floor of the entrance hall below me. Above I could hear Paul still singing when the warders, roaring with rage, entered his cell. Legraverend and I got away with it, but Paul was given three days in handcuffs. Rather to our surprise, the matter went no further and we all felt that we had been let off very lightly. The general discipline of the prison had certainly been relaxed.

Legraverend and I worked on our system of secret correspondence until it was perfect. We were now allowed to receive parcels every two weeks instead of once a month and, as his day for parcels was different from mine, this meant that one or other of us received news from outside every week. My laundry was now being collected and searched in my cell by an elegant young lieutenant. I had noticed that when my linen was really filthy, he would pick it up with the tips of his fingers, holding it as far away from himself as possible, with nostrils averted and an intense expression of distaste on his face. From that moment I saw to it that my laundry was always disgustingly filthy; so much so, indeed, that he made me fold the things and put them in the suitcase with my own hands. This was just what I wanted, for I could now send home the equivalent of ten quarto pages of manuscript at a time. I wrote, of course, in the tiniest possible writing on sheets of thin notepaper from very small notebooks. Few people could have read the characters as they were. For once my shortsightedness was of some use. My parents unpicked the seams of my laundry when it arrived, took out the sheets of paper and read the tiny writing with a strong magnifying glass.

Our food-distributing system was working very well too. Now that more parcels were allowed in, some of my comrades were able to eat better than they had done for months. I received a regular supply of eggs and I used to pass some of them to Paul up the pipe for wider distribution beyond. When Paul pulled his string up through the pipe, with the parcel at the end, I always held my hand across the pipe in case the string should break and the parcel fall back down the pipe past me and on down to the cellars.

On the other hand, no string was necessary when delivering

73

food to Legraverend in a cell a floor below me. I simply let the parcel slide freely down the pipe. Legraverend would stand on his table with his hand thrust up into the hole in his pipe, waiting for delivery. I tried first with a piece of sausage, which was a great success. It fell through the space which separated us, and arrived at high speed in his hand. I sent him various sorts of food in this way. But things went wrong one day when I sent him a hard-boiled egg. Half a second after I had let go of the egg I heard an angry roar, then a loud bump from the ground floor. There was the noise of a fall, and then a great deal of shouting in German. Paul and I listened anxiously, standing on our tables, our ears at the heating pipe. At last there was silence. I called down nervously:

'Jean-Marie! Have you hurt yourself?'

'No. Call you later. Being watched.'

Two hours later, when coffee time came, Jean-Marie called me back.

'Hullo, Pierre. Well, old boy, you know what you did? That egg wasn't cooked properly. It broke in my hands and at that very moment the sergeant came in. I just had time to throw myself off the table, and pretend I had been cleaning it. But of course, there I was with egg all over my hands. It wouldn't wash! Three days without a mattress!'

We did not know, as we laughed over this, that our friendship was soon to end. On 9 July 1943—I remember the date very well, because it was exactly two years to the day since my arrest—Jean-Marie Legraverend was taken away. We hardly had time to say goodbye to him and to wish him good luck.

Part Two

I

One brilliantly sunny morning at the end of October of that same year, 1943, a warder came to my cell and told me to report for medical examination. This always took place before transfer to Germany and I had already suspected that some move was in store for me. When I lined up for the doctor in the main hall, I was amazed to see my uncle, Bernard de Francqueville, in the queue. I had not even known that he had been arrested, far less that he was in the same prison. I was shocked to see the pallor of his face, but he was still smiling in his usual way. He seemed to be accepting everything that was happening with his characteristic simple good humour. His air of quiet confidence and optimism obviously had a good effect on those around him.

After a brief examination we were all passed as fit. I felt almost sure that we were going to a concentration camp. The only question was when and where. In fact it was not until three or four weeks later that the move took place. I was summoned to the hall with about thirty others and I was pleased to see that my uncle was amongst them. As we stood there, holding our few possessions, we felt in good spirits. We assumed for some reason that we would be going to the camp at Compiègne, which we had heard had an excellent reputation. Later we discovered that this was totally undeserved. Thousands of Jews were sent there on their way to their deaths at Auschwitz; but we did not know this at the time. In any case we nearly all agreed that wherever we were sent must almost certainly be a change for the better. My uncle was the only one who reserved his opinion. He had come into prison from the outside world much later than I had and knew more of what had been going on. Not wishing to depress us, he said little, but it was clear that he was apprehensive about what lay ahead. However, prescient though he was, even my uncle did not know what we were about to face.

We had to wait in the yard for some time and were able to talk quite freely because the guards were not on the alert. This was a tremendous, almost overpowering experience for me, for I had not talked face to face with anyone for more than two years. Nor had I stood for more than a second or two as one of a group. The mental excitement soon began to tell on me. My head ached and I felt sick and dizzy, as a child might feel after too many rides on the roundabouts at a fair.

Our personal possessions, watches, fountain pens, pocket-books and so on were formally restored to us, according to lists which had been drawn up. My pocket-book and pen, which were not returned, had probably been stolen by the police when I was arrested; but I did get back my watch.

After this we were made to have showers and were disinfected. While waiting for the prison van to arrive, we were shut in little cells only large enough for two people. As we crossed Paris packed into the back of the van, it was heart-rending to have those tantalising glimpses of the old familiar world, to be so near and yet so far. I remember, too, seeing a few discontented, surly faces and wondered how men and women who had their liberty could look anything but gay and happy.

We arrived at the station and, heavily guarded by about forty policemen, we were hustled into a third-class coach, five to a compartment, and locked in. The windows were barred. The German police got into the coach with us, but the French, who did not seem to be enthusiastic about their role, came no farther than the platform. It still did not occur to me that there was something sinister about the size of our escort or the thorough-ness of the precautions that were being taken to ensure that none of us tried to escape. We were only thirty in number, after all, and at least ten of us would not have had the strength to escape even if we had been presented with an easy chance. My suspicions should have been aroused.

One fine feat of French courage and resolve lit an otherwise dark day. On the opposite platform a railwayman in blue overalls walked slowly up and down, staring nonchalantly into our compartments. Quietly he made a sign to us with his hand, which we rightly took to mean that we should write a message and throw the paper out to him. Some of my companions, when the police were not looking, were able to do this and I learned later that all those messages reached their families. I greatly admired the cool courage and spontaneous comradeship of that railwayman, who took such a risk under the very noses of the German policemen.

We were all, apart from my uncle, still certain that we were going to Compiègne. But as the train moved off it became clear that we were not. Night fell and, as the train gathered speed towards the mysterious and threatening east, our jokes and laughter died away and we fell silent. Pressing our faces against the windows, we watched the peaceful, isolated lights which winked in the darkness as they floated past us. In the morning, before dawn, we crossed the frontier. One of us tried to croon: 'Nous repasserons bientôt dans l'autre sens,' but no one listened to him. In our hearts we were already saying to ourselves: 'It will not be better. Perhaps it is going to be harder than ever. You will have to gather all your strength if you want to live.' As the last lights of France grew dim on the horizon, each of us seemed to turn his gaze in upon himself and silently follow his own thoughts. When silence falls on men in such circumstances it is a burden in itself. For they choose to be silent in order not to communicate their fears, and each man being silent knows what the silence of the other man means.

And so we were when we came to our destination. It was still dark when we arrived. Blue lamps shed pale circles of light on the empty platform. I remember how suddenly a big fellow in a steel helmet, his rifle on his shoulder, moved out of the shadows where he had been invisible and strode into the circle of light, his iron-shod boots ringing on the shining tarmac. A squad of S.S. men came into sight some distance up the platform. They hurried down to our compartments and unlocked our doors.

We had arrived in German territory. From the moment we first set foot outside the train we realised the difference. We were now forgotten men, theoretically dead. Even at that moment there, on the station at Saarbruck, I began to ask myself if it would not have been better to be really dead. I had many mad thoughts in my worst moments at Fresnes. But I had never been so insane as to have thought that one day I would sigh for the peace of Fresnes and regret that I had left it. But at Saarbruck I was to look back on that cell in Fresnes as on a haven. What irony there is at the heart of tragedy! No wonder the Greeks believed that man is not the beloved creation but the plaything of the Gods.

We had hardly stepped out on to the platform when the S.S. fell on us as if they had gone berserk. Yelling like lunatics, kicking and pummelling us, they chained us into couples, and then drove us like cattle into a long line. In the confusion one of the prisoners, an old general, fell down. It was obvious that he had injured himself badly; in fact afterwards we discovered that he had broken his arm. The S.S. stood over him and kicked him until he managed to get to his feet. We huddled up together like sheep surrounded by wolves, clutching our spare clothes and Red Cross food parcels and wondering what was going to happen next. Then an order was given and we were hounded off into a covered lorry.

How we survived the four or five mile journey to the camp I shall never know. The S.S. crammed twice as many men into the van as I would have thought possible. To get enough clearance to enable him to pull the doors across, an enormous S.S. man grasped the sides of the door panel with each hand to steady himself and kicked at us until we squeezed ourselves back into the van. By the time we reached the camp, we were all in a state of near collapse and three men were unconscious. When we tumbled out of the prison truck, it was full daylight, a pale, grey, autumnal day shrouded with a wet, clinging mist. The bitter cold knifed into us as we emerged from the van, which naturally had been as hot as a furnace.

Neue Bremm, where we had arrived, was a Reprisal Camp. It was small compared with Dachau or Buchenwald and was designed to house only about a hundred and fifty prisoners. Only a dozen or so S.S. men were needed to look after it, for it was little more than four hundred yards square. Its function was to knock prisoners about so much that, by the time they left to go to a concentration camp, all the spirit had gone out of them and they consequently required only the minimum of supervision. In view of the shortage of German manpower, the supervision of prisoners had to be done with as few guards as possible.

On two of its sides Neue Bremm was bordered by roads. One was fairly large but little frequented; the other, which was more of a lane than a road, was used only by peasants and labourers. The camp was fenced with barbed wire, which was not, however, electrified; and there was a look-out tower at each corner. Nearby there was, of all things, a country pub called 'The Black Eagle'.

Having scrambled out of the lorry, we were made to stand in a line outside the administrative building, our faces to the wall, with orders not to turn round. We were still in our prison clothes or whatever clothes our parents or friends had been allowed to supply us with. The plain black suit of the professor, intended to be worn with a dignified stiff white collar, the young man's sports coat and the priest's cassock must have looked most curious in these surroundings.

Then we had our first roll-call. As each man's name was called, he answered and stepped into the barrack room. Here, when my turn came, I was ordered to hand over all the things which only a few hours ago at Fresnes had been solemnly returned to me. I also had to give up my Red Cross parcel. I was left with only the clothes I was wearing. After a short interrogation to verify his identity, each man left the building and returned to his position facing the wall.

As I stood there I was given my first introduction to our new

79

way of life, and in particular to a feature of it which we later came to call the Circus. I remember being almost stupefied by the sight, although I took care that my face still appeared to be turned towards the wall.

Imagine a bare, open space, surrounded by barrack buildings. In the centre was a kind of pond, the depth of which was perhaps ten feet at the middle and at the sides not more than two or three. About twenty men of various ages were running around this pool. Two S.S. men were looking on and grinning, while about half a dozen young men in prison uniform stood around, armed with truncheons. They were hitting at the others as they ran past, flogging hard at anyone who did not keep up the pace. The prisoners with the truncheons, we soon discovered, were young Ukrainians. They had become 'hommes de confiance', 'trusties', hangers-on, servants, batmen, to the S.S., and as long as they treated their masters like gods and the other prisoners like cattle, they were privileged. So they wielded their truncheons energetically, flinging themselves on anyone who flagged, reviving fainting energies and tired muscles with enthusiastic assaults.

It was a pathetic sight, which would have been comic if it had not been horrible. For when the blows fell, the runners would increase their pace, pretend to go all out. In fact they did their best to conserve their energies for, as we ourselves were to discover only too soon, to go flat out might be fatal. You might overdo it, collapse and fall, and then one of the S.S. would finish you off in whatever fashion he chose.

As we stood there, still watching out of the corners of our eyes, the weather changed. A cold, dry wind came up. It blew away the clouds of early morning, and a pale sun rose to light up the scene. The twenty men ran on. Suddenly one of them—God knows what he was trying to do—broke away from the line, and ran falteringly towards the barracks. He just managed to get to the wall and collapsed, exhausted. An S.S. man walked in a leisurely way over to where he lay, stood there and, hands on hips, began to shout down at him. There was no response. The S.S. man started to kick him. We heard the groans as the poor fellow returned to consciousness, and gradually he struggled to his knees. As he swayed there on his heels the S.S. man hit him hard and neatly in the face. He went out cold. The S.S. man wiped his knuckles carefully with his handkerchief and came over to where we were standing.

I was terrified. If this was how Neue Bremm was, I certainly could not survive. I knew enough of my physical and psychological condition to recognise its limitations. The years in prison had weakened my muscles and had put a dangerous strain upon my heart. The mere noise of conversation with my comrades in the yard at Fresnes, the very freshness of the air, had made me feel giddy and I had nearly fainted. One look at the Circus and I felt that I would not be able to take much more.

My comrades and I continued to stand like dummies, petrified, facing the wall in the corner of the barrack square. Meanwhile the others went on running around the pool like automatons, their bodies stiff, their faces twisted into inhuman masks.

Eventually one of the Ukrainians came up, carrying a stool. Our heads were to be shaved in the standard camp pattern, which was a sort of cross, one line sideways and one lengthways across the scalp. Each of us in turn sat down on the ground, while the Ukrainian sat on the stool and shaved us. Once this was done, we were marched off to our barrack room. Beyond the entrance hall of this building there was a long central room where we were to sleep. There were two tiers of bunks on each side of it, about forty in all. On each bunk there was a mattress made of sacking, which had once been filled with straw; but the straw, never having been changed, was now flattened to practically nothing. There was a stove in the middle of the room and a few rough benches round it. What light there was came through narrow windows set high up at either end of the barrack room.

It must have been about eleven o'clock when we entered. We had only been there a few minutes when the main door was flung open to the accompaniment of a roar that I shall never forget. Instinctively we stood to immediate attention at the foot of our beds. The man who now stormed in on us was Le Négrier, the slave driver, so nicknamed by our predecessors. He was not big, burly and coarse-looking, as one would imagine. He was about fifty years old, thin and frail, grey-haired and of less than medium height. His face was long and pale, the lips very thin and straight, his general appearance insignificant. Only his eyes gave a clue to his nature; they were black and deep set and they burned with a light that suggested something of the fanatic. At times the pupils dilated so much they seemed to shoot from his head, and his face would be contorted by a peculiar kind of tic which simultaneously jerked his right eyebrow up and the left hand corner of his mouth down. We soon discovered that the appearance of the tic showed that his temper had soared to boiling point. It was the danger signal.

Having begun with his extraordinarily frightening roar, he continued in a perfectly calm tone of voice to give us our orders. They were translated for us into French by a Ukrainian. The essential rules of camp discipline were explained to us. First, every order was to be obeyed at the double. Ordinary walking was completely forbidden. Secondly, the blast from a whistle meant that all prisoners must double to the barrack square and stand to attention awaiting orders. Le Négrier, having given his instructions, turned on his heel and left.

We were just beginning to tell each other that this S.S. man at any rate seemed comparatively inoffensive and that therefore life in the camp might be better than our experience at the railway station had suggested, when we heard a blast of the whistle. We hurled ourselves out of the door, jostling and hustling to get through first. On the other side, waiting for us, were two S.S. men, armed with truncheons. They started beating us as we came through, and chased after us, raining down blows, until we were all standing to attention on the edge of the parade ground, just outside our barrack room. We were starting our life at the reprisal camp of Neue Bremm as we were meant to go on.

The Circus was still in action. They were still running around the pool as they had been when we arrived. An S.S. man was shouting at one prisoner, who was outside the line, to sit down and stand up in rapid succession. At the 'Sit down' order he threw himself on the floor, stomach down. We watched, still and silent. Then a new command was bellowed out. Everyone in the Circus, including the single prisoner, dispersed, running as fast as he could to the blocks. We too were told to march back from the square to our barrack room. The square was left empty.

As we marched the few strides back to the hut we saw that one prisoner, a great skeleton of a fellow, with his clothes in tatters, did not run. He shambled along with big strides, swinging his arms loosely from the shoulder like an ape. He disappeared inside one of the blocks, only to reappear immediately, staggering under the impact of kicks and blows. He caught sight of an S.S. man strolling across the square and limped over to him, standing to attention very respectfully, beret in hand, and seemed to ask permission to do something. The S.S. man, laughing coarsely, answered by pointing in the direction of our block. The man ambled off at his strange pace, half-walk, half-run, and came over to our barrack room. By now we ourselves had gone inside. He passed quite close by me. The poor fellow was obviously crazy. He looked at us with an expression both kind and absent, as though he saw not only us but something we could not see. Then he gazed around him in silence, as though surprised to find himself there.

Suddenly, outside the hut, there was the same mad roar of rage which had terrified us earlier on. At the sound of it the prisoner began to tremble but did not move. Le Négrier stode in, carrying a horse-whip. He was in a transport of fury, of pathological rage, his eyes bulging from his head. He hurled himself on the prisoner with all his strength, beating him about the head, yelling at the top of his voice, his mouth twisted, his dreadful tic shooting up and down his face. It was all over in a few seconds. The wretched creature had stumbled out, the voice sobbing, the long arms waving in vague broken gestures.

Le Négrier, still in the same state of dementia, came back, foaming at the mouth. It was absolutely forbidden, he screamed at us, for any outsider to enter our barrack-room. We must turn out anyone who tried to come in or we would be severely punished ourselves.

Then, though no one had done anything to provoke him, his anger turned on us, who were still standing at the foot of our beds, stupefied by what we had seen.

'Pigs!' he yelled, 'you are the enemies of *das Grösser Reich*. Our Führer will know how to deal with your filth, your beastliness, your cesspools of countries. Do you hear me, sons of pigs?'

The word pig and its derivatives held a high place in his vocabulary. Naturally we said nothing. Suddenly, in a new access, he seized a stool, and hurled it across the room at the prisoners opposite. No one, as it happened, was hit. His anger left him as quickly as it had flared up. He went as white as a sheet, and, muttering vaguely, he turned and hurried out of the room.

We were flabbergasted. As soon as he had gone we drew into small groups and discussed what we had seen. A prisoner called Martin and my uncle Bernard were nearest to me and began talking about it. But I could hardly say anything, hardly listen to them, because I was thoroughly demoralised. How was I going to run, crawl and jump with a crippled leg, and what would happen to me if I didn't? I stood there dazed and dumb with fear. Martin turned to me and tapped me gently on the shoulder. His calm, pink face surveyed me kindly. I did not see his white hair cut into the four ridiculous tufts. I only felt the strength of his body, short-legged and robust, and the warmth of his eyes, full of irony and kindness.

'Well, well, my boy; now what's the matter with you?'

I smiled and murmured something vaguely. It was difficult to tell Martin that I was so afraid. And, anyway, I felt a little better.

Later I got to know Martin well. He was over sixty, a socialist of the old school, a purist and a syndicalist. He had fought against the British on principle in the Boer War. Later he had spent a year as a prisoner of war in a camp in Ceylon. He baffled the Germans. They simply could not make out how a man, whom the British had put in a prisoner of war camp, could choose twenty years afterwards to risk his life in their cause.

Martin was remarkably young and vigorous-looking for his

age. He always wore the cap he must have worn at home, and it gave him an especially youthful air. He had a great sense of humour and even when things looked at their blackest he could make us smile at our own anxieties with his gentle teasing.

My uncle's background was in complete contrast. He had led a comfortable and easy life. He was a rich man, and except during the 1914–18 war, in which he had fought bravely, he had never had any material problems. His existence, orderly and tranquil, had been passed between work and the simple pleasures of family life. As a professor of international law he could hardly be said to have equipped or prepared himself for a career in the camps, much less for the Circus. He also was deeply depressed by the events of the morning.

'They can destroy our bodies, but not our spirit,' said Martin. 'We are living proofs of the spirit and they can do nothing against us.'

'Living proofs of the spirit . . . living proofs of the spirit,' muttered my uncle, with the kindly, sardonic half-smile so typical of him, and his head on one side. But I felt a moment's pride at the sound of it.

2

Fear easily displaces the appetite for food. Only now at about noon, twenty hours since we had eaten our last meal at Fresnes, were we sufficiently recovered from our stupefaction to become conscious of our hunger. We realised this when one of our group, whose turn it was to maintain a surreptitious watch at the window which gave on to the barrack square, announced that large pots were being brought out. A few minutes passed and then there was a blast on the whistle.

This time, as we rushed out, we practised what was to become a familiar technique, so quickly does fear make you adapt to new situations. As we neared the door we bent low, hunched our shoulders and put our arms over our heads. It was an undignified posture, especially for Generals of the Army and professors. Nor did it offer complete protection, but the amount of damage sustained was at any rate much reduced. Other prisoners were pouring out from other blocks in exactly the same way.

The whole camp of about a hundred and fifty men fell in and stood to attention. Out of the corner of my eye I could see that the block next to us was made up of Frenchmen. Some of us recognised friends and colleagues, and stealthy signs of recognition were exchanged. In the general confusion over collecting our food, many of us were able to say a hastily whispered word to comrades in the other French block. Judging by the orders issued, most of the prisoners in other blocks were Russian.

On the other side of the square a few S.S. men, surrounded by the Ukrainian hangers-on, were standing around a steaming pot.

A few yards off another S.S. man stood behind a trestle table on which tin bowls were piled. A second man stood behind a counter where there were piles of sliced bread. Another group of S.S. men stood in the doorway of the administrative building, smoking cigarettes and looking on. They appeared to be anticipating some sort of entertainment, to judge by the way they shook with laughter every now and then and slapped their thighs.

Each of us in turn went up to the bread counter to receive one slice about half an inch thick, smeared thinly with margarine and jam. We then moved along to be given a tin bowl, and then to the group of S.S. men who stood around the pot, one of whom filled the bowl with soup.

Now the sport began. As I have explained, everything had to be done at the double. The prisoner, therefore, had to return at the double to the sanctuary of his block, carrying his bread and soup and knowing that, if he slowed down to prevent the soup from spilling, he would be thrashed for disobeying camp orders. To provide more sport for the onlookers, three big Ukrainians, armed with cudgels, were posted between the serving benches and the barrack-rooms.

The more agile, more practised or simply more fortunate of us could reach our blocks without losing more than a drop or two of soup. But most of us lost between half and all of the only hot food we were to receive during that twenty-four hours.

The Russians were much better than we were at adapting to this strenuous operation. They simply poured the soup down their gullets as they ran. It was done in a few seconds. But in order to succeed in this one needed a Russian gullet and a Russian stomach. It was not very funny. Several times I saw veterans of the First War and distinguished professors weep with rage and humiliation when they were back in their blockhouse contemplating an empty bowl.

We were no more than playthings and laughing-stocks to those sadistic and perverted brutes. Nor had we yet understood that it was their policy to demoralise us by making us look utterly ludicrous to each other; and this was almost more important to them than the brutality to which we were being systematically subjected. Suffering, in certain circumstances at least, gives dignity and therefore a kind of strength. It is the feeling of being a lunatic that disintegrates and deprives one of the capacity to be oneself. At the end of half a day I felt emptied of every thought and desire save that of keeping going at any price, and of conserving my strength, which I felt was already ebbing away.

The only comfort was to feel oneself in the company of men of character. Although we hardly knew one another, there was from the outset an atmosphere of comradeship. No man thought of himself first; there was a sense of common sympathy, of understanding, sharing, and a general assumption that we must help each other at all times. I think it was due to the exceptional moral quality of those men. The bond was not fear but love. There is so much love when circumstances call for it, when our shyness and conventional distrust of each other and of ourselves is swept out by the wind of harsh reality.

I remember old General G., who had been trampled down and had broken his arm when we arrived on the station at Saarbruck. He must have been nearer sixty than fifty. Yet he not only managed, his arm in a sling, to keep up with us in the insane pace of our daily round, but he was able also to smile, and say good-humoured, encouraging things to those who were on the point of despairing, and to laugh at himself as much as at the S.S. Martin, the oldest and perhaps the most serene of us, also saw humour in everything. He could cheer us at all times by making us laugh. His presence was always a great comfort, and his fine example made me ashamed of my lack of courage. I squared my shoulders and pulled myself together as I realised that I was almost young enough to be his grandson. I noticed more than once that it was the elder men who set the best example.

Not that any of us had much time to think of our misfortunes. Hardly had we swallowed our lunch on that first day, when the whistle blew. Again the stampede, again the cudgelling at the door, and again we were standing to attention in the square.

We now made the acquaintance of Trokur, the most interesting man at Neue Bremm. We had already learnt, from remarks dropped by those who had been longer at the camp, that the two worst S.S. men were Le Négrier and Trokur. Le Négrier was abnormal, sadistic, fit for a lunatic asylum and a strait jacket; but Trokur was even stranger, for he knew perfectly well what he was doing and why. I only learnt his story after the war. It seems that before the war he had been a butcher who ran a successful business in Saarbruck. He had had the reputation of being sensible, hard-working and kind; a good fellow, a worthy citizen, and a pillar of the local community. Every morning he was to be seen proudly taking his daughters to school, walking hand in hand with the little blonde pig-tailed girls. At his trial, after the war, nothing could be discovered in his past to explain the sophisticated and elaborate cruelty which he displayed at Neue Bremm. Perhaps the thoroughness with which he implemented the reprisal camp policy was the result of a simple determination not to lose a comfortable and convenient post. After all he was in a very fortunate position. He was doing his war service on his own door-step. He was able to keep his eye on his business in Saarbruck, and, when he felt like it, go down to his house, have lunch or dinner and make love to Madame. At the trial, neighbours who were called as witnesses testified that in this most united and domesticated family, it was Madame, not Monsieur, who wore the trousers.

Trokur was a little above medium height, but very thickset, strong, cunning and cold-bloodedly brutal. Like Le Négrier, he had an insanely explosive temper. When roused, he would go red in the face, his eyes would bulge, but unlike Le Négrier he remained sane.

His massive body was unexpectedly swift and supple, and he would spring upon you when you least expected it with amazing speed. He liked to get each man on his own. The W.C. was one of his hunting grounds. As a rule, in both reprisal and concentration camps the W.C. was the one place where there was a trace of privacy. But it was never safe from Trokur, who had a habit of lurking there. Fortunately there was one W.C. not far from our block, but it was difficult to reach it without being seen. If one succeeded in doing so, one was safe more often than not. But sometimes when one was squatting there, congratulating oneself on one's good fortune, Trokur would appear unexpectedly, wearing rubber-soled boots or bedroom slippers so that his approach would not be heard on the concrete. Then of course one was trapped. The cudgel blows fell on head and shoulders, and one was kicked on the buttocks and in the groin to the sound of ecstatic cursing and shouting. Many who entered that W.C. never came out alive. Other poor wretches would crawl back to their blocks on hands and knees, covered with blood. I suppose this perverted and sadistic man enjoyed the element of the chase and the thrill of the stalker, as he stealthily tiptoed to the W.C. after his victim. And I think that the discomfiture and humiliation of the man he surprised appealed to his twisted sense of humour.

One day a prisoner, who was probably slowly dying of hunger anyway, fainted while he was working outside the precincts of the camp. He was brought back that evening, hardly conscious, lying at the bottom of the lorry in which the labour squads were transported. We were running round the pond at the time and I could only see out of the corner of my eye what happened when the lorry pulled up inside the camp. An S.S. man hauled the prisoner out by the leg and dragged him across the yard to a shed near the administrative building. He bumped his head over the ground all the way. The door of the shed remained open, which enabled me to see inside every time I completed a circuit of the pool. The poor devil had been thrown on to a solid-looking table. The next time I ran past I saw that Trokur was gripping the man's head by the hair, lifting it up as far as it would go from the neck and banging it back rhythmically on the table. Two or three S.S. men, who must have been told what was going on, had crossed the square to the shed and were now laughing at the scene. Trokur was red and furious, and banged the man's head harder and harder on the table. This went on for about ten minutes and then the door was closed. The man was never seen again.

The whistle sounded again some time later, when we were back in our barracks. It was almost dark by now and icy cold, as we hurled ourselves out through the doorway of our block for about the tenth time. In the half-light we saw to our astonishment stark naked men come running out of the neighbouring blocks and make towards a building about three hundred yards away at the other side of the camp. An S.S. man yelled at us to undress and join our comrades at the bath house. This we promptly did, though even in that fearful moment I could not help thinking what a comic sight we must have been.

Here there was no question of avoiding the cold water douche which lasted for three or four minutes; nor the race back across the square, wet and naked, to our block. It was December and the pond around which we ran was already covered with ice. I should never have thought it possible that any of us could survive such a régime. But the human body is tougher than one supposes.

After the shower we stretched ourselves out on our palliasses, fully dressed and with our shoes within reach in case at any moment that terrible whistle might sound again. And indeed the day was not yet over. There was still the evening roll-call, which took place indoors. We were always ready to spring to our feet to minimise the risk of provoking Trokur, who usually conducted it. We had already decided that one of us must always be on watch at the window to warn the others of his arrival. Once the roll-call was over we were left in peace.

In a piercing voice and an appalling accent the Ukrainian who accompanied Trokur began to call out our names on the register. While this was going on Trokur smiled and casually filed his nails. This made a curious impression on us, but we took care to look completely blank, for we already knew how important it was to keep the atmosphere calm. When the Ukrainian came to the end of the register, he cried out in a coarse bellow: 'Good . . .' Afterwards we learned that the prisoners were supposed at this point to roar at the tops of their voices the regulation, 'Night.' At this Trokur would elegantly click his heels and salute with his great, soft hand. It was a hideous, perverted and mortifying pleasantry which I can hardly describe. But on this first evening, since none of us knew the drill, the 'Good . . .' was followed by complete silence. Trokur, surprised by this, stopped filing his nails. Then as he realised what had happened, his face went purple. He roared abuse at the Ukrainian, who in his turn abused us and taught us the response. The lesson was repeated about a dozen times. Then we were left in peace.

An uneasy, menaced peace, hardly worthy of the name. Martin was snoring steadily after a few minutes, but the rest of us were not so fortunate. I was lying beside my uncle and soon I felt the comfort of his hand upon my arm. In the darkness he whispered:

'We must pray. Will you pray with me?'

I asked no questions; I simply asked God for His help and support, speaking to Him as one speaks to a friend who is always ready to listen and in whose power of comfort one has no doubt. I prayed, forcing my lips to form the words. But all the time my ears were straining to catch any sound in the camp, and my eyes were searching the shadows for unknown dangers. Hours passed in this way. I could not sleep.

About midnight, when I believe I was about to doze off, a sort of scratching noise just outside the barrack-room awakened me again. Then I thought I heard rapid steps pass down the centre of the dormitory. I got up in the half darkness, for there was a full moon shining brilliantly, and ran barefoot down the central alley between the bunks. One of my comrades had had the same idea. We tried to peer out of the casement window, but it was too high. K. cupped his hands together and made a foothold for me. I stepped up and looked out on to the deserted square. The ice on the little pond stared back shining in the moonlight like a large sad eye. I was just about to step down when the faint scrabbling sound was repeated, not more than a yard or two away. I peered hard into the black shadow thrown by our building. There was the madman, the wandering Russian with the beret, who had entered our barrack-room, against the rules, earlier that day. Now he was there just beneath me, leaning with one hand against the wall, the other hand holding a piece of bread to his mouth. He munched quietly and with relish, moving his head up and down, and back and forth, making what I think were little murmurings of satisfaction, as though he were enjoying his meal.

A door slammed, and the Russian flattened himself against the wall, invisible. He became quiet as a mouse at once. The door of the next barrack-room had opened and a figure had slipped out furtively and was creeping away towards the W.C. A prisoner was risking a meeting with Trokur. Just at that moment I had to get down as K's hands were giving way. We changed places.

As he got into position a cry of pain rang out, followed by shouts in German. K., taken by surprise, nearly slipped from his perch, but I held him steady. Our comrades were awake at once with the noise outside. The shouting continued but it was punctuated now by a dull moaning.

'The swine!' I heard K. say with great intensity and I felt him shudder.

He got down, his eyes large with horror, and in a low voice which controlled his emotion he described what happened. The man had evidently only reached the door of the latrine when Trokur, whom he had not heard approaching from behind, knocked him down. Trokur then got hold of him by the leg and dragged him the full length of the barrack hut, before leaving him prostrate on the ground. K. and I crouched by the window, listening. After a few minutes he made a foothold for me and I raised myself on to his shoulders. There was nothing to be seen. The courtyard was empty. Trokur had disappeared, probably into the administrative building or to prepare some other ambush, and the man whom he had beaten up had apparently dragged himself back into his hut.

Meanwhile there had not been a sound from the Russian. I looked everywhere for him and at last located him in the shadows. He was lying full length, with his head pillowed on the old bag which he always carried with him. He would be there all night, it seemed, in the bitter cold.

Everything was quiet now. Across the square, beyond the opposite barrack buildings, the moon shone in a streak of light on the barrel of a machine gun. It was mounted on the flat roof of the look-out tower and its mouth pointed down towards us.

We both went to bed. Our first day had come to as near a close as was possible at Neue Bremm.

3

It was still night when the whistle blew. At once there was a wild rush to dress and get to the door. In two minutes I had scrambled into my clothes and helped my uncle. As the first men raced through the door of the block, Trokur burst upon us. Obviously he had been on duty all that night. His eyes were bloodshot and he bellowed and brandished his truncheon. As I went by he swung a blow at me. I ducked and it glanced off my uncle's shoulder, bruising and shaking him. As Trokur lashed out around him, another of our comrades, a Belgian, was knocked out. The rest of us ran on and in a few minutes we were all standing in the courtyard under the floodlights, which the guards in the look-out towers had directed on to us.

My uncle and I and about a dozen others were told to leave the ranks on the square and group ourselves by the main doorway of the camp. The choice seemed to have been made at random, and we waited in a good deal of anxiety, not knowing what might be in store for us. We knew enough about this hellish place by now to realise that the most unpredictable things might happen. All that seemed evident at the moment was that we were to leave the camp. Our fears diminished a little when, with the usual shower of blows and kicks, coffee was dished out to us. They would hardly give us coffee before we left for our unknown destination, if we were to be shot or beaten to death. We waited at attention for another half-hour. Meanwhile the rest of our comrades had started the Circus. Such was the nightmarish quality of this place, that one seriously asked oneself if they had ever stopped running round the pool, or if any of this could really be happening. Then a lorry arrived and we all got in.

The journey was a short one. Through chinks in the sides of the lorry I could see that we were passing through rich agricultural land, although in this weather and at this time of the year it looked dull and sad. We stopped in the middle of fields beside a solitary ploughshare, which a casual bystander might have assumed had been abandoned to the wind and rain. The new S.S. man, who was to remain in sole charge of us, explained that we were to be harnessed to the plough and were to drag it back and forth over the field, turning the earth to a depth of fourteen inches. The field was to be finished by the evening.

It was not easy, for we pulled unequally against each other. Two horses would have done it better. The field seemed endless. It must have been a strange sight to see a dozen men, their backs bent, dragging the plough in the dawn over the desolate field under the low, rain-charged, late November sky.

As soon as the lorry had disappeared over the sky-line, we made the only pleasant discovery that I remember during those terrible days at Neue Bremm. The new warder was not like the brutes in the camp. Once he was sure that the truck was out of sight, he left us to ourselves. He installed himself in a sheltered corner of the field, from where he could keep an eye on us. Then he un- packed his provisions and settled down to make the best of a dreary day. It was clear that, so long as the work was done by the appointed time, he would not bother us. We arranged a system of working in shifts, which allowed some of us to rest at the other end of the field. We made the most of this respite, while our guard rolled and smoked cigarettes, and called out to the heavy, blonde- haired land girls who were working in the adjoining fields.

Near a hedge was a large heap of rotting cabbages. We took it in turns to lie concealed behind the heap and pick out those not yet too rotten to eat. They may not have been very nourishing, but at least they filled our stomachs and took away that feeling of emptiness which was nearly always with us, and which was worse than mere hunger. All the most shocking pettiness, all forms of cowardice and the most degrading kinds of selfishness become possible when one is *really* hungry. We gobbled up those filthy cabbages with gusto, crouching in the shelter of that rotting heap whose smell alone in normal circumstances would have made the idea of eating repugnant.

If we could have gone to the field every day, life at Neue Bremm would have been different. But that was the only occasion when I was lucky enough to be picked for that work. It was work which was eagerly sought, because neither Trokur nor Le Négrier went on these country expeditions. The old hands of the camp always tried, under cover of the half-light of dawn, to slip into the group of those who were chosen. But most of those who played this game got caught sooner or later. And when a man got caught he was beaten up in real earnest. Even if he managed to survive the beating up, he was always the object of special attention afterwards. Sooner or later this almost certainly ended in his death.

It was at Neue Bremm that I first came in contact with Russians. They were very impressive. They had such resilience and easy courage. Nothing got them down. They were nearly all young, of course, and this may have had something to do with it. We could not speak to them often because they lived in a different blockhouse, and in any case there was the language difficulty. They seemed to like the French and to treat us as allies. Whenever they got a chance they smiled or winked at us, as though we were partners in crime or virtue. They were wonderfully good-natured and optimistic. Now and again, at the shower or at meal times, they gave us to understand through signs and simple words that Germany and Hitler would soon be '*kaput*'.

'*Ja, ja*,' we answered, and we would all laugh together.

They were honest, straightforward men, whom one could imagine living a very different kind of life. They reminded me of the two young painters in Dostoievsky's *Crime and Punishment*, who did their work singing and whistling, while upstairs Raskolnikov killed the old usuress. They were like puppies, able to

96

pass hours romping together and amusing themselves with nothing. But there was also the other side to their character, when I saw them as irresponsible, sentimental, sometimes desperate and brutal.

I remember one of them in particular. He was a young soldier, whose name was Piotr. Like the rest of his compatriots in the camp, he was quite small, short in the back, with well-knit, solid muscles and a square, bony head with deep cavities. One day at the shower, when there was no S.S. guard present, I managed to explain to him that our names were the same. He made me repeat Pierre once or twice and then went off into a great burst of uncontrollable laughter. I suppose he found it comic that the same name should be pronounced in two totally different ways.

His story, which I pieced together by gestures and from the few words we had in common, was the story of thousands of Russians captured by the Germans in the very first days of their attack on Russia. Isolated by tanks from the rest of his unit, Piotr and a handful of comrades were able for an hour or two to continue firing and throwing grenades from good cover on tanks passing down the main roads. But they were eventually located, raked with machine-gun fire by aircraft, encircled by troops and forced to surrender. He told me of the long and terrible march across the plains of Russia. Snow started to fall when they reached the Polish border and one by one his comrades fell dead by the wayside. Following behind in a wagon were a few German soldiers whose duty it was to finish off those who could go no farther. From time to time the dry report of a pistol was heard, half muffled by the snow. The survivors arrived at last in one of those immense camps in which thousands of prisoners had already been herded together; men of every region, every faith, every rank and calling, a vast conglomeration of races, European and Asiatic. The barracks, put up in haste to house a twentieth of the numbers now forced into them, were hopelessly inadequate, the hygiene conditions appalling. Men died like flies.

Piotr summed up the situation and decided that he preferred to run the risk of dying from exposure in the snow than face inevitable extinction by disease. He spent two nights in the

97

woods without daring to make a fire lest the smoke during the day or the flames at night should betray him. On the third morning he was spotted. After a short chase when shots whistled around him, he was recaptured. Piotr was put into a goods wagon with forty other escapers. For a week the train shunted, coupled and uncoupled, stopped in stations and sidings and eventually arrived at a little West German town, clean and tidy as a new penny. The prisoners were badly and rarely fed during the halts, so that their hunger made them beat and kick at the partitions. When they arrived they were bruised and exhausted, and as filthy as cattle going to slaughter. Dazed by the daylight and the difference in the landscape, they emerged from the wagon haggard and tottering, with eight days' growth of beard. They were herded into an enclosure already occupied to bursting point by several hundred others who had also tried and failed to escape. The camp was strictly guarded and was surrounded by an electrified and double barbed-wire fence. On the four look-out towers, day and night, stood guards with their fingers on the triggers of their machine guns.

Piotr was not in the least discouraged by the failure of this first attempt to escape. As soon as there was the slightest chance he tried again. I have no idea what motives or hopes lay behind his incredible optimism and tenacity. His reactions were always so unexpected. I think he may have been driven by a kind of vital necessity to find his own people, his own kind of life, an air in which he could breathe naturally. Later I noticed in other Russians this same passion, profound, exclusive and blind, to get back to their own land. It explained the mad courage with which they would risk all to make a run for it. Piotr was, of course, completely ignorant of time and distance. If he had realised that, in order to find his comrades, he would have to cross almost half a continent, perhaps he would have given up his project.

Anyway, he tried his luck once more. Carefully built tunnels and elaborate escape routes were all very well for the French and the British, and even for the Americans; but the Russians, especially simple peasants like Piotr, found simpler solutions. As soon as a suitable occasion presented itself, a Russian would seize it without counting the cost. One day when he was doing outside work in the woods with a dozen others, Piotr slipped into a thicket and stayed squatting there until nightfall. It was less than an hour before the escape was discovered, but it was not until the following night that he was recaptured, as he crept round a farm searching for food. If his hunger had not forced him to move out of his hiding place too soon, he might have evaded his trackers.

He was condemned to two months at a reprisal camp and this was when he came to Neue Bremm. He had already served most of his sentence there when I arrived, and when the time came to leave the camp, he and I left in the same convoy. I had noticed that for a day or two he had been less communicative than usual. I felt that he was planning something, but I did not dare question him. In any case he probably would not have confided in me.

At our departure there was none of the ghastly treatment we had been subjected to on arrival. Many internees have recorded that once prisoners had received a thorough conditioning on Neue Bremm lines, the S.S. seemed to relax their treatment. Now, instead of the usual animal truck, we were to travel in a fairly comfortable third-class carriage, which we boarded at Saarbruck. I found myself sitting next to Piotr. I can still see his severe face, with its strongly marked features just visible in the dim light of the compartment. He remained silent, morose even; and his face was heavy as he stared vacantly out of the window. The rest of us, ignorant of what awaited us, were delighted to leave the hell of Neue Bremm, and the atmosphere in the carriage was almost gay. We organised games under the paternal eye of our new gaoler who, to our surprise, was not an S.S. man. Piotr stayed scornfully in his corner. At last our carriage, pushed by a shunting engine, was attached to the train. We pressed like flies against the window to catch a glimpse of civilians travelling on the train. But in the poor light of the blacked-out blue lamps we saw nothing more than a few shadowy figures battling against the wind outside.

The train started, and at once the geography experts began to calculate in which direction we were travelling. The wildest hypotheses circulated. We had been going for perhaps an hour when the train, which was already moving slowly, puffing and gasping for breath, reduced its speed still further and, above the noise of the wheels and the conversation, I heard quite clearly two or three bursts of firing. The talk ceased suddenly. The train had stopped right out in the countryside. The night was dark, the sky covered with clouds, so that we could see nothing.

A red-faced soldier came to our compartment to check the occupants against a list he held in his hand. It was at this point that I saw that Piotr was no longer in his seat next to me. For some reason the soldier was slow to realise that there should also have been a Russian with us, and by that time the train had started again. It was not until it stopped at the next station that he was able to get out and telephone. I never knew what became of Piotr. Even if he had managed to jump from the train without hurting himself, he had almost no chance of escaping. He was probably recaptured and taken back to Neue Bremm, where he must soon have died of ill-treatment.

But to return to our life at Neue Bremm. Day by day, as a result of the Circus, the beatings and the absence of food, we were becoming physically weaker. Nevertheless, our morale was excellent. I do not think that any of us lost courage. Some still had the strength to laugh, and above all at themselves. But for the last few days of our two weeks at the camp, we lived in a semi-stupefied condition, hardly aware of the grotesquely horrifying character of our lives. To stay alive was good enough. We were becoming, as we were intended to become, increasingly passive; aware only of certain vital necessities of which food was the most important. We would be almost overcome by a kind of violent despair if by accident or clumsiness we lost a few drops of our precious soup. Stealing into us too was an unhealthy hatred of those who, more adroit than ourselves, had managed to preserve their soup ration on occasions when we had spilled our own. At Neue Bremm, as opposed to Buchenwald, this hatred never showed itself. But I well remember feeling it.

One day we were all together in the barrack-room, awaiting the blast on the whistle. I was near the door, watching the mad Russian in the beret who continued all day and every day to wander from block to block, vainly seeking a refuge. I was counting my blessings, telling myself how much more fortunate I was than the Russian, in that I belonged to a human group which made life seem less insecure, even if it were not. Suddenly the door opened and Trokur appeared. I was only a few steps from him.

'I want two men,' he shouted.

He did not seem to be in a particularly bad temper, but to shout was part of his nature. We knew that this was the signal for those nearest the door to rush forward as 'volunteers'. This I did, cursing my ill luck in happening to be there. Another man, Lherbe, whom I was to know well later on, also ran forward. We followed Trokur, who on this occasion seemed to be more or less at peace with the world and was whistling a waltz tune. I felt dozens of pairs of eyes fixed on us sympathetically, as we crossed the square to our unknown job. It was amazing how much better I felt in consequence.

Trokur led us to a barrack hut where a young Russian boy, who was obviously very ill indeed, lay dumped on a rotten mattress. He was only a heap of bones and a foetid smell rose from him. Trokur began to shout at him until he turned his head very slowly towards us. All my life I shall see that look empty of feeling, all emotion extinguished, a look with nothing there. They had burned off his eyelids.

Even Trokur seemed affected. He merely grumbled something about 'filthy pig' and ordered us to lift him up. Evidently they had left him some days without attention, for the smell caught one by the throat. Trokur was muttering: 'Get on, get on.' The young Russian could hardly move his legs, and they certainly would not support him. The skin of his forehead seemed black, and as we got near to the door and the light I saw that this was due to blows which could only have been recent.

We were not going fast enough for Trokur, or perhaps he thought we were taking too much care. We had placed the young man's arms around our necks so as to be better able to carry him.

As we crossed the square we tried to jerk him as little as possible, feeling the life so weak in him. This was the moment Trokur chose to start kicking the dying man. We were passing the administrative building and it was probably a matter of prestige in the eyes of his fellows. I think much of the brutality I saw in the camps was caused by men trying to prove to each other that their nerves were proof against the ghastliness of their own deeds. And this only drove them on to further feats of cruelty. I felt the echo of the blows in my own body. Lherbe and I would far rather have received the kicks ourselves, instead of feeling the thud of them landing on this poor tortured body, even though by now it hardly reacted to them.

At least we were across the courtyard, and Trokur opened the door of the shower room. We were to wash our comrade and change his clothes. We took off the filthy rags. I thought the cold douche would kill the boy. I can see him now, sitting on the ground, his arms, without muscles or flesh, still somehow able to support him. We washed and dried him as gently as possible, then carried him to the camp stores where a shirt and trousers were thrown at him. When we dressed him, he seemed a little better, more alive, and in spite of his tortured face he found the strength to give us a sort of dreadful smile. His swollen lips opened and we saw that he had no teeth. A sort of gurgle escaped from his throat. Trokur kept telling us to hurry. We had to be quick so as to avoid further blows falling on him. When we had carried him back to the barrack hut, we lifted him on to the bed. He was gasping for breath and the sinister gargling sound was still coming from his throat. Perhaps it was the beginning of the death rattle. We left him there and never saw him again.

A day or two later we left Neue Bremm. On the whole we had come well out of it. Things could have been worse. We had only been whistled out on to parade on average three or four times a night. We learned later that either by chance or design we had not been treated as badly as some who had been at the camp before us. After the war I found that nobody had survived more than fifty days of the full Neue Bremm treatment. A few of our group had died, a few had gone mad; but those who were left felt that they would now be able to face anything. Nothing could be worse than the physical ordeal we had just undergone. Our capacity to face such an ordeal had been augmented, and indeed transformed, by the satisfaction of feeling that we formed one heart and one soul. When we were reunited in the evenings in the dusk of the barrack-room, it was as though a united family had reassembled. We had stood together in the ordeal, one for all, all for one. Differences of political views, race, religion or class had ceased to matter.

We left Neue Bremm in good heart, not knowing our next destination. Perhaps we would not have been so cheerful if we had realised that we were bound for Buchenwald.

4

We arrived at Buchenwald at two o'clock in the morning, a few days before Christmas of 1943. It had been snowing and a faint moon, not strong enough to reveal objects but bright enough to make the snow gleam, shone down on the great, white, sparkling plain. It was a still and peaceful scene. We had no idea that thousands of people lay in bunks close around us, and that the vast expanse of twinkling whiteness, which stretched away into the distance, was not a plain but the parade ground of the camp of Buchenwald.

We were still standing there two hours later when the scene changed. For the first roll-call at Buchenwald took place at about five in the morning. At the sound of the whistle clusters of tiny black dots appeared on the horizon, miles away as it seemed, and converged up the slopes to form into groups and march towards us in regular patterns. Huge floodlights snapped on all around and above us. Then out of the silence came the unexpected and grotesque blare of a brass band. Now we could see both the size of the camp and the numbers it held. Squad after squad, twelve abreast and twelve deep, strode past us to take up their positions for the roll-call. They marched arm in arm to support those who were too weak to walk on their own. Each man looked ghostly. The remnants of every uniform in the world, it seemed, hung on their starved bodies; and these tatters carried the dirt, slime and refuse of years.

The roll-call, which was compulsory before starting the day's work either inside or outside the camp, generally took one or two hours. Most of the prisoners who died in the camp did so while waiting in the snow for their names to be called. The evening roll-call at six o'clock was the worst ordeal, because the men were exhausted by the day's work and were often too late back to the camp to have had the evening meal. We stood and watched. Even we, who had seen much in the last two years of captivity, were staggered by what we saw. Meanwhile the band played with enthusiasm and as though at a village sports day. There were sixty instrumentalists in bright red uniform that had once belonged to the Bulgarian royal band, and they ranged through a whole repertoire of waltzes, gavottes and marches.

By the time this first roll-call was over it was daylight and we were able to see the camp. Buchenwald camp was near the city of Weimar in Thuringia, East Germany. It was ironic that it should be so near to the town where Germany's main democratic experiment, the establishment of the German Republic in July 1919, was inaugurated. It was also a town which had been a leading cultural centre in the nineteenth century and had been especially associated with Goethe, Schiller and Herder. There had never been a town or village at Buchenwald. It took its name from a high, flattish expanse on which a famous forest of beeches once grew. A few trees remained, including the historic 'Goethe's Oak' under which the poet was said to have sat and meditated. The camp was exposed to the most bitter winds, which were to become worse in January and February. They seemed to come direct and unimpeded from the North Pole.

When Buchenwald was first established it was fairly small. It only expanded as time went on and more use was made of it. The main gateway, with the famous 'To Each His Own' motto above it, was set in a long, low stone building in which were the quarters for the guards and the administrative offices. It was surmounted by one of the main watch-towers equipped with searchlights, guards and machine-guns. The parade ground immediately inside the gate was large enough to hold tens of thousands of men. Beyond it were the prisoners' blockhouses, mostly constructed of wood. An electrified fence surrounded the camp. There were numerous other stone buildings for offices, stores, bath-houses and so on.

After the roll-call had taken place and the parade ground had been cleared, our small group was marched to the admissions block. There we were told that we would be medically examined, de-loused, registered and issued with camp clothing.

Registration at concentration camps was a highly important business. Once your number had been assigned to you, you existed only as a number. There were cases on record of men being flogged because their numbers had been confused with other men's, or because by mistake a dead man's number had been reassigned to them. We were told to put down our things and strip off what we were wearing. I had a fur jacket which my parents had sent me. I put it down, feeling certain that I would never see it again, and I was right.

We entered the de-lousing block. Here an orderly ran an electric shaver all over our bodies as though we were sheep, removing every single hair. Next we were sprayed with fine powder. Then we had to run at the camp double—everything had to be done at the double—to the bath-house. This was a huge, barn-like stone building, which had been built with prisoner labour. It stood about a hundred yards away from the de-lousing block. I remember standing there waiting for the water to shoot out of the nozzle of the pipe without any sense of apprehension. I suppose many thousands of others stood under such nozzles in other camps, equally unsuspecting, waiting for the water to come out and realising only at the last moment that what was coming out was gas. Indeed through most of this hour it was surprising how unapprehensive we were. No one was beaten up and, although there was roughness, there was no deliberate brutality as at Neue Bremm. The water in the showers was tepid instead of freezing cold, and this greatly increased one's feeling that things were taking a turn for the better.

Our camp uniforms were issued next, thrown at us, regardless of size or shape, as we passed in front of a counter. At the same time we were issued with triangular coloured patches to indicate to what category or nationality the prisoner belonged. His number on a small tab had to be sewn under the coloured patch. My number was 21,521.

We were then sent out into the open air. It was terribly cold and the air bit into us cruelly after the comparative warmth of the bath-house. Stupefied, I looked at my ill-fitting uniform with its ridiculous, humiliating stripes, and at the clumsy wooden-soled boots. I looked down in dismay at my number tab which, although there was no needle and thread, must obviously be sewn on if I were not to be beaten. I remember so well how I felt: dazed, lost, directionless and above all completely anonymous. The number in my hand was the only token of my identity, my very existence. When I left Fresnes I had had a feeling of something like elation. In spite of all my failings and failures I had managed to stand a great deal. There had been a similar sense of confidence when I left Neue Bremm; a feeling of pride that the horrors we had experienced had welded our little group together with a sense of comradeship which lifted us above ourselves. Now as I stood there looking down at my number tab, I had a horrid feeling of dissociation from everything, a feeling of dehumanisation which was difficult to analyse. This was probably what I was intended to feel and I had a sickening fear that I might succumb to it.

I do not know how long I would have stood there staring blindly at the rough camp uniform in my hands and that scrap of material with my number on it. But within a few minutes we were ordered to fall in and march to the quarantine block. Here the block leader harangued us for several minutes about camp discipline. He was a prisoner himself, a communist, who had been in the camp ever since it had been built. Nearly all the internal administration and organisation of the camp was in the hands of such senior prisoners, who were in their turn responsible to the S.S. This huge brute of a man howled at us as though we were idiots, a habit many of the Germans had. He repeated his text over and over again that if there was no discipline in the camp we should *all* die. He made it clear that he and his fellow prisoners at the top of the camp hierarchy had no intention of dying. Any indiscipline or lack of co-operation on our part would meet with the severest punishment, not excluding death. Death from our fellow prisoners.

We were in the quarantine block No. 43 for a couple of weeks. The temperature at night was fifteen degrees below zero. We were dressed only in underpants, light-weight jackets and trousers. There were about three hundred of us in the building and when the roll-call took place we huddled together as closely as we possibly could. What an incredible sight it must have been, that mass of human flesh, swaying slightly to keep its balance and trying to keep itself from freezing to death.

Two weeks later we were moved to a standard type block, Block No. 26. This was a large, rectangular building with windows set high up in the walls, just below the point at which the roof began to slope. The entrance was half-way along one of the sides. Immediately inside the door were the washing place and lavatories and a few small rooms for the block leader or Kapo and his deputies. These were the favoured few, the Stubendienst, the 'trusties' who had the privilege of doing the easy fatigues and the prerogative of fetching the food. To the left and the right of this open area were doors leading to the two main chambers formed by the small block containing the rooms.

My group was told to turn off to the chamber on the left. Here the bunks were arranged in three tiers along the length of the short wall. There had once been straw palliasses on the bunks, but by the time I arrived at Buchenwald you were expected to sleep on plain wood. Two men slept head to foot on each bunk and, as these were very narrow, your partner's feet were almost in your face. Each main chamber contained about a hundred bunks, so that the total population of the average blockhouse, including the Kapos and their hangers-on, was about five hundred men. In front of the bunks was an open space where there were benches and tables; and, better still, there was a brazier in which burned a large fire. We were exhausted by the cold of the last fortnight and, as this hut was luxurious in comparison with the quarantine block, we lay down and slept. Our normal routine at Buchenwald had begun.

The block leader blew his whistle at four o'clock the next morning, which was the normal hour for reveille. Our first duty was to wash from the waist up. A huge wash bowl, six or seven feet across, was fixed on the floor in the open part of the chamber in front of the bunks. About twenty-five men would jostle each other and wash at it at the same time. The Kapos stormed at us to make haste so that we should be out on parade in time for the S.S., and they threatened us with beatings if we got them into trouble. There was no soap, but later on one or two of us managed to scrounge some or were sent tablets in our Red Cross parcels. There were no towels either, and the water was very cold. We were warned that, unless we used the lavatory immediately before or after we had washed, we would not get another chance. There was no privacy at the lavatories, which were just a row of about ten bowls. We queued up and the lucky ones managed to get to one before we went out on parade. The rest had to wait until night-time. Everything was subject to the overriding importance of the squad being on the parade ground for roll-call at the right time.

We now rushed back to the main chamber, where we were ordered to sit on benches at the rough tables in front of our bunks. Our breakfast of coffee and bread was brought in, the coffee in enormous urns. Each man was given a mug holding about half a pint. The so-called coffee was really a kind of dark-coloured water. That first morning I thought the breakfast frightful, but in comparison with what we were to have later it was good. I was able to eat as much bread as I wished then, but there came a time when we were reduced to a single round of bread. This bread which we were issued with at breakfast was the last food that we would have until the evening.

We were only allowed five minutes for our breakfast and then we were ordered to form up in front of the block. Our block leader now put himself at our head and we marched up the small road, which ran past our blockhouse to one of the main roads leading to the parade ground. Dozens and dozens of other squads were marching towards the Appelplatz, all under the brilliant glare of the floodlights.

As we arrived on the parade ground we came under the scrutiny and within the range of the S.S. I witnessed none of the deliberate sadism that I had seen in Neue Bremm; but out of the corner of my eye I could see that those prisoners who from fatigue or illness were slow in taking up their positions were harried by S.S., armed with clubs, or by one of the dozens of specially trained dogs who patrolled the camp. In some of the squads marching past us two men were holding up a third man between them. I thought at the time that this was because he was too weak to walk, but in many cases it was because the man was dead. Everything in the camp depended on the roll-call. Sick or well, alive or dead, you attended the Appel. Those who had died in the night had to be hauled up to the morning Appel, then off to work, and back again in the evening for the final reckoning. You could not die, officially, until *after* the evening roll-call. It was much easier and safer for your friends to produce your dead body than to try to explain to the S.S. why you were not there to answer your name at the end of the day.

That particular morning roll-call lasted about three-quarters of an hour. This was about the average. If there were a hitch of some kind, or if one squad had arrived with a man short, the roll-call could last several hours. I often stood in the snow for five hours and I believe there is a record of one Appel lasting for more than a day.

After the Appel was over the Kapos in charge of the commandos or labour gangs took over and the day's work was organised. That first day no one bothered about us much. We were not assigned to any of the commandos, but did odd jobs around the hospital and kitchens.

These left me with a rather hopeful impression of what life at the camp might be like. So far as the hospital was concerned, if a Red Cross inspection team had come to look over it, they would have gone away very reassured. The beds, equipment and the state of cleanliness were adequate. There were good doctors of all nationalities. I was to discover that it was possible to have very good dental treatment at Buchenwald. But before you went to the dental centre it was as well to make sure that you were going to be cured and not liquidated, either in the course of an experiment or because a fellow prisoner acting as dental orderly had his knife into you.

The camp kitchens were also admirably equipped and the standard of hygiene in them was magnificent. An International Inspection Team would have been equally satisfied with them, as they would with the selected blockhouses to which they would have been taken. Here they would find bunks equipped with mattresses, good fires burning in the open area in the main chamber, and scrupulously kept lavatories.

5

The second meal of the day, the evening meal, was served about seven o'clock. We were given a kind of stew. Compared with what we were to get later it was not at all bad. My dish contained eight or nine pieces of potato and even a few bits of meat. Again, you had to hurry through the meal because the Kapos were concerned to get you out on the parade ground for the evening Appel. We now saw the disadvantage of being on an out-of-camp working party. Several men from our block who had been working in the quarry arrived back late. When they paraded to march the two miles home, somebody seemed to be missing. The S.S. refused to move off without him and there was a search. As was so often the case, a mistake had been made in calling the roll, but it took an hour to find this out. Meanwhile the whole squad of about a hundred men had been kept waiting. They arrived back only a few minutes before the Appel. There was no time for them to eat their food. There was enough left over for them, but by the time we finished with the Appel and they got back to our block, it had become cold, rancid and unappetising. Later in the war, there was so little food that if you arrived back late there would be none left, and you would go out to the Appel starving.

Roll-call that night did not last very long, an hour and a half perhaps. And afterwards we were free to do what we liked until the whistle blew at four a.m. Those of us who had not been sent on the heavy commandos were not very tired and our curiosity about the camp kept us mentally active. We began to compare notes and to question those of the veterans who seemed reasonably friendly and communicative. The majority of the inmates of the block soon went to bed, some exhausted with the day's work, others exhausted not so much by work as by pessimism and tedium. A few played cards; one or two read books. There was a small library in the camp, but few prisoners were prepared to stand for a long time in a queue, only to receive the first volume that the librarian pushed into their hands. There was a showing of a film about once a week, but again one had to wait a long time to get a ticket and few men were ever in the mood to go.

By listening to others I picked up a certain amount of information about concentration camps in general and Buchenwald in particular. The great majority of prisoners were either German or Russian. Most of the camps had originated in the early thirties as places where those Germans who publicly or secretly resisted the Nazi régime could be 're-educated'. Torture, beatings and solitary confinement usually taught them to moderate their opposition and then they would return to normal life. Many were tortured in order to obtain confessions or information. The more recalcitrant ones would be detained or liquidated. The camps were also used for criminals. When the war came, and particularly after Hitler's victories in the East brought in thousands and thousands of Russian prisoners, they were also used as prisoner-of-war camps. This was not officially disclosed, however, because prisoners-of-war were entitled to altogether better treatment.

In Buchenwald at this time, we learned, there were a great many veteran German communists and socialists. Most of these had been in concentration camps since the Communist Party had been banned after the burning of the Reichstag. The legal basis of the camps had been established by the Enabling Act of 1933, by which the Chancellor was allowed to govern by decree if he declared a national emergency.

There were also a great many German priests and ministers in the camp, men whose religious views had led them to resist the Nazis in public. Some were Roman Catholics, some Protestants.

Among the most determined of them were the Jehovah's Witnesses. There were also many Jews, some of whom were undergoing sentences because they had married or had had sexual relations with Aryans. An increasing number were there just because they were Jews. Another very large group was made up of criminals of all kinds, varying from thieves to rapists, from black marketeers to homosexuals. There was a minority of spies, prisoners-of-war, or political prisoners. Amongst these there were only a very few who, like me, had been members of the French underground. On the whole the different categories of prisoner were kept in separate barracks, although they were frequently mixed in the labour gangs. As the war dragged on, certain camps were used as liquidation centres, where Jews were killed by the thousand. But this was never done on a big scale at Buchenwald.

The internal affairs of these camps were run by the prisoners. The German personnel, which consisted mainly of the S.S. guards and one or two doctors in the experimental block, were kept down to a minimum. In fact the whole idea of the *concentration* camp was to be able to hold down masses of prisoners with as little supervision as possible from the Germans. Discipline in the blocks, staffing of the hospitals and kitchens, organisation of the labour commandos, were all in the hands of the prisoner-bosses, the Kapos. When the main portals of the camp were shut at night, apart from a few guards manning the machine-guns and searchlight on the watch-towers, the camp was entirely a prisoner society.

As the war progressed, the camps were swollen by the influx of prisoners, while the provision of military guards to maintain control of them became more difficult owing to the increasing demands on German manpower. Concentration camps, therefore, came to be more and more controlled, not by S.S. guards but by a deliberately created atmosphere of terror and demoralisation. It was the especial function of reprisal camps like Neue Bremm to frighten, humiliate and dehumanise prisoners by beating, starving, and, above all, degrading them. We were not, for instance, even allowed to have paper of any kind for use in the lavatory. Prisoners not only lost any power of initiative or resistance, but also even the will to live. This made them much easier to keep in order.

In most of the camps, I was told, there was a considerable tension between the various groups of prisoners, a tension which to some extent the Germans encouraged because it made the camp easier to control. Tensions were usually greatest between the two categories which were then easily in the majority, the communists and the criminals, the Reds and the Greens, so called because of the colour of the distinguishing patches on their uniforms. In some camps the criminals had got themselves the top jobs, but in Buchenwald the communists had established themselves as masters. They were in a majority there in its early days, and had used their positions in the camp administrative offices, kitchens and hospitals, to promote the interests of their own group and undermine those of the Greens. They arranged things so that members of their own network received better food and were given the lighter jobs. They were able to keep them out of the really heavy 'killer' jobs, such as the quarry, the railway and (strangely enough) the flower and kitchen gardens. They also organised it so that tough criminals or political enemies who resisted their hegemony would, if they went near the hospital, mysteriously contract illnesses which ended in their death.

While I was sitting in my block, listening to the general talk, one of the block Kapo's lieutenants came up to me and told me that two prisoners were looking for me. I walked away from the group and in a moment or two these men, Kogon and Hummelsheim, came up to me. They told me that they were Roman Catholics, and that I had had the good fortune to be put into a block whose Kapo was also a Roman Catholic. They knew my name and told me that before they had been put in a concentration camp some time before the war, they had been members of the German Centre Party and had been on friendly terms with my father. They warned me that it was essential to act most cautiously in the camp because I was under suspicion. The top communists who controlled the camp suspected that I had right wing political connections. I must watch my step, therefore, or I would endanger not only my own life but that of any other prisoner with whom I appeared to be on good terms.

They explained how easy it was to become unwittingly involved in the rivalry between the communists and other political parties, since the communists and their allies had always to struggle to maintain political supremacy and the power over life and death within the camp. Every now and again there would come a request for a forced labour draft for some distant place. The communist labour Kapos would try to exclude their supporters from the lists they submitted, and their enemies would try to include as many communists as possible. Much of the struggle went on behind the scenes and underground. Both sides tried to get their men into any job in the camp which could provide direct or indirect influence. If they could get them into the kitchens, they could get food which could be used for bribing. In the offices they would have access to files and to the lists which were drawn up for forced labour. In the medical blocks they could obtain drugs to cure or drugs to kill. The camp, they warned me, was an extension of the underground which I had known in France, a jungle, a no-man's land, except that here you knew even less who was on whose side and could be sure that both sides knew all about you. My main danger was not from the S.S., brutal and indifferent to life and death as they were, but from my fellow prisoners. All newcomers like me were carefully studied to see to which political way of thought they belonged.

I said I thought it extraordinary that any of my fellow prisoners should be suspicious of me. I had after all fought hard against the common enemy and suffered a good deal in the process. They replied that, although the communists in the camp would do anything to bring down the Nazi régime, they had very little regard for Roman Catholics of upper-class origin. These they considered nearly as much the enemy of international communism as German capitalists and Nazis. They would do everything they could to consolidate their power within the camp, with the object of using that power against capitalism when the war was over. Everything they did was seen in those terms, and life and death within the camp was distributed with that object in mind.

My new friends also told me that, although he was friendly to me, my block Kapo was apprehensive in case the communists who ran the camp should put a black mark against my name. In this case he and his colleagues would not wish to be too closely associated with me. My best policy was to keep as quiet and inconspicuous as possible. They left me feeling rather worried.

Like the other newcomers, I did various fatigues around the block for a couple of days. Then as we were about to double out for Appel one morning, one of the assistant block leaders came up to me and handed me a small chit of coarse paper with a signature and a rubber stamp mark on it. It instructed me to report that morning to one of the leaders of the camp Arbeit-statistik, or labour office. This man was one of the most powerful prisoners in the camp. He was responsible to the S.S. for the organisation, supply and deployment of labour within the camp. The S.S. did not bother themselves with the selection and detailing of individual prisoners. They simply told the Arbeitstatistik how many men were required for a particular place at a particular time, what the project was, and how long it would take. The head of the Arbeitstatistik, through his clerical staff of prisoners, selected the individuals.

The Arbeitstatistik headquarters was on the far side of the parade ground near the main gate of the camp. I went into the outer office and a clerk took my chit and read it. He walked over to the door, knocked, and in I went.

This was the first time for more than two years that I had been in a living-room, indeed any kind of a room, with the exception of the interrogation room at Fresnes. It had a peculiar effect on me which I recall very well but cannot analyse, though it was certainly overwhelming. The man I had come to see sat in a leather armchair, smoking a cigarette and reading a newspaper. This was the first time I had seen a newspaper for eighteen months. He was dressed well, almost elegantly, in riding jacket, breeches and boots, shirt and tie. He looked clean, fresh, well-groomed, whereas my clothes were foul-smelling and filthy with the effects of two or three days' fatigues. Already I was beginning to think of myself not as a man but a number. He motioned me to one of the chairs. The last time I had sat in one had been at Fresnes when I had been interrogated. On a small table there was a box of cigarettes from which I was invited to take one. It was extraordinary, like a dream.

The man was T., one of the most memorable men I have ever met. He began to talk to me in a friendly, conversational tone, as the head of a firm might speak to somebody scarcely junior to himself whom he was thinking of offering a very senior post or even a directorship. He was tall, well-built and broad-shouldered, with a hard but intelligent face, handsome and determined. His manner was relaxed and quiet. He had been sent to Dachau, the earliest camp of this kind, when he was seventeen, and had been in the camps ever since. Whereas my number was 21,521, his was around 100. In the eleven years which he had spent in about as tough and competitive a society of men as could be imagined, he had risen resolutely to the top. At twenty-eight he was a veteran leader and a most impressive man.

His questions to begin with were so casual and conversational that they were hardly questions at all. We talked about the part of France I came from, where I had been to school, and whether I had enjoyed life at the university. He asked me how I got on with my father, whether I had had a happy childhood, whether I had been spoiled or whether I had been encouraged to make my own way and to think for myself. We must have talked together for more than an hour, at the end of which time he suggested that I should come back the next day. He went over to his desk, wrote something on my chit, signed and stamped it, and returned it to me. This chit, which I still have, said that I was to report to him at the same time every day until further notice, and it excused me from taking part in any of the labour squads.

My Kapo did not say much when I showed him the chit. Other men in the block, however, were deeply impressed. T. was so high in the camp hierarchy that he made contact with only a handful of the tens of thousands of prisoners who passed through his files at one time or another. His orders were transmitted to three or four assistants, who in turn worked through junior commanders; they in their turn worked through the Kapos. It was unheard of in my block for T. to interest himself in an individual prisoner, let alone invite him to the comfort of his room and chat to him over several cigarettes. Some of the men in my block thought it all very suspicious. Others thought I was singled out for privilege.

I arrived there early when I reported back the next day. Some prisoners, who had been found malingering, were being paraded in front of the Arbeitstatistik. T. appeared from his rooms dressed only in his breeches and singlet. He snapped out his criticism of them, and then began to hit out at them deliberately and scientifically with his fists, using them as a boxer in training uses the punch bag. He kept it up for about ten minutes. Every man got a drubbing, and three men were knocked out cold. T. threw a towel over his shoulders, on which a little perspiration had risen, and went to his shower. The episode did not seem to have given him any sadistic pleasure, nor on the other hand had he shown the slightest sign of temper. I saw him do this several times in the succeeding days. He seemed to regard it in a matter-of-fact way as a convenient combination of disciplinary action and vigorous exercise.

When I was called in to his sitting-room on the second day he was as neat and relaxed as ever. He greeted me affably, offered me a cigarette. After my talks with my friends in the block the night before I realised that I must be very cautious. But there seemed nothing to be on guard about. T's manner was good-natured and frank. Now and again he would become a little more probing, a little more persistent, but only, it seemed, because something I had said had not seemed clear. I could not always see the point or direction of some of his questions, so I took them all at face value and answered them truthfully. I was able to answer all his questions about the underground with perfect candour because, as I said to him, all the information would now be out of date anyway. I still do not know whether he was much interested in any of the specific answers to his questions. Perhaps he was really probing to find out what kind of a man I was and whether I was dangerous or harmless.

Looking back on these talks, I realise now how long it must have taken him to make up his mind, because so many of the incidents of my upbringing must have seemed contradictory. For instance: (against) educated by the Jesuits, and coached for the military school at St. Cyr; (for) later, prepared for the Ecole Normale Supérieure, and being wounded by the police when demonstrating against the Government during the Stavisky affair in 1934.

This second session was again a long one. At the end of it he rose to his feet, went to the desk, handed me back my chit, and sent me off.

My daily visits, all similar, continued for the next ten days or so. There was only one incident that stood out. T. always sat with his back to the window and I sat in the chair immediately opposite him. The window looked out on to a part of the camp between the administrative buildings which was rather off the beaten track. One morning as I was answering his questions, my gaze wandered past his to the window. I saw that a lorry had drawn up some thirty yards away. Men were unloading corpses from the truck and were throwing them into what may have been some kind of burial pit. This unloading of corpses went on for several minutes. I watched, fascinated but, so far as I was aware, I gave no indication of what I was looking at. It was at this point that T. began to talk to me of the dangers which befell those who would not learn what he called 'the lessons of the camp'. One must learn these rules quickly, he said, and obey them carefully; otherwise destruction was inevitable.

Afterwards I wondered whether he had deliberately arranged for me to see the lorry being unloaded, and whether he had made a bid to frighten me into saying something which would reveal me in my suspected true colours.

At the end of the final session, however, he handed me my chit and said quite casually:

'You need not come tomorrow.' It said I was now available for work in the normal way.

It was not until many years after that I knew the full meaning of this episode.

While I was still in prison at Fresnes, I was of course totally ignorant of what was being done for me. I had in fact been sentenced to death, and, thanks to the efforts of a number of people belonging to what the communists would have called reactionary circles, had eventually been reprieved. My father had sought and obtained a personal audience with a certain French cardinal. Cardinal B. told him flatly that people in my plight had nobody to blame but themselves, and that there was nothing to be done about it. My father persevered. Though he was well known in France and Germany as a critic of Nazism, he was equally well known as a friend and admirer of the German people. Roman Catholic scholars and writers in occupied countries became acquainted with his efforts to get me reprieved. The Pope and General Franco had been approached. Ultimately, Madame de Kallay, wife of the then Hungarian premier, took up my case. Apparently, she got into personal contact with Hitler and obtained from him a promise that the death sentence, of which I had known nothing at the time, would not in fact be carried out. As a special favour my life would be spared and I would be sent to Buchenwald instead. What Madame de Kallay and my father did not know was that no German who knew anything about the concentration camps would have regarded being sent to Buchenwald as a reprieve. At best it meant that the official German authorities had announced that I would not be formally executed as an enemy of the Reich.

By the time I reached the camp T. knew all about this. The names of people like Madame de Kallay who had spoken on my behalf had been entered on my documents. T.'s clerks reported to him that I was a protégé of high-powered Roman Catholic reactionaries. T. had gone some way towards making up his mind that I was a potential menace; but fortunately for me there was another prisoner in the camp who had enormous influence. This was Eugene Kogon, a German who was also a Roman Catholic. Kogon was a man of immense culture, with a great love of music and literature, greatly respected in the camp by people of all parties. He was in fact in a powerful position and was able to influence the camp hierarchy very considerably.

Kogon was familiar with my father's books (anti-Nazi, and which had been destroyed by the Nazis after the fall of France), understood his general attitude to Germany, and was convinced that I was not in fact a Roman Catholic reactionary. When he learned that the communist hierarchy had decided to liquidate me as soon as possible, he spoke up on my behalf. 'Pierre d'Harcourt is all right,' is what he said in effect. 'He is a simple patriot. He may not be one of us, but he is not one of them.' He continued to press my case with T. during the period of the latter's interrogations of me.

T. was sufficiently impressed by Kogon's advocacy on my behalf to take the trouble to vet me personally. If he had had any doubt about me after talking to me for several days, he would have given me a harmless looking chit instructing me to report to the medical block. Before long, perhaps on the pretext of giving me some treatment for my wounds, which were troubling me all the time, one of his agents would have given me an injection. That would have been that. But T. was a just man. He 'tried' me systematically, patiently, and conscientiously, for fourteen days, and discharged me. He had my life in his hands and spared it.

After the war was over, I heard somehow, somewhere, that T. was in East Berlin and had a post with the government there. I wrote to him. Eventually my letter reached him, and he replied. It was an interesting letter, neither perfunctory nor revealing, very guarded in anything that at all touched or might seem to touch on politics.

It ended with the cryptic sentence: 'I hope, Comrade, you will remember the lessons of the camp.'

6

For the next three or four days I continued to do light fatigues around the block. After that I was to be posted to one of the permanent labour commandos.

During this short period I picked up a great deal more information about camp life. Prisoners who were considered fit enough for work were assigned to one of a variety of occupations. First there was the quarry, which provided the stone for repairs and extensions within the camp, as well as for the building of workshops outside the camp. Squads went out each morning at the double and did not return until the evening. They would march the two or three miles there and back, as well as having to work long and exhausting hours in the quarry. The workshops for which they quarried the stone were used for the repair and production of military equipment of various kinds. They were really subsidiaries of several important factories in the region. They were constructed along the six-mile long concrete road built from the camp to connect it with the main road to Weimar. This was known as The Street of Blood on account of the number of prisoners who had already lost their lives while working on it. Both this road and the railway which ran alongside it had been built by prisoner labour.

Within the camp were a few specialised workshops. In one of them optical instruments were repaired for the German Navy. In another socks were knitted by machinery. Several prisoners were employed in minding this machinery. It was an extremely comfortable job which only those who were well in favour with the prisoner overlords were ever likely to get.

Great quantities of fuel were required in the camp for the kitchens, workshops and crematoria, and many prisoners were more or less permanently engaged in hauling coal or coke. There was also a permanent force at work in the camp gardens, for vegetables as well as flowers were grown at Buchenwald to be sold at a good profit to the people of Weimar. At the time I arrived in the camp a number of prisoners were being employed to dig up and remove the roots of trees which had been felled earlier on when the camp had been extended. There was also a pig farm, to which prisoner squads were assigned, and here again the meat was sold outside.

From time to time drafts of prisoner labour, nominated by the prisoner labour bosses, were requisitioned and despatched from the camp temporarily to work elsewhere. Some were transferred permanently to other concentration camps, from which they supplied German war factories with labour. The most dreaded of these were the underground plants of Dora, Ellrich and S.3.

All work was paid for. Payment was made in camp currency, which theoretically was to be spent in the camp canteen. In fact camp money was practically worthless. Real money, a bit of gold from a dead prisoner's teeth, or a fur jacket stolen from a dying man, or any other such articles were most valuable. You could buy practically anything in the camp canteen, if you had the wherewithal. Prisoners who worked in the S.S. stores and canteen and who had contacts in Weimar procured a great range of goods which they disposed of in the camp black market. The top prisoners and their hangers-on could buy every kind of food and drink, including champagne and caviar.

You could even buy women. The camp was provided with an official brothel, to which any prisoner was free to go. The women prisoners who made themselves available there were of three kinds. There were those who had been politically active, or who had been the wives or mistresses of political activists, and who wanted to give their male colleagues the consolation of sexual intercourse. Others offered themselves in the brothel because they wanted sexual intercourse for themselves. A third kind of woman went there to give her services in return for privileges or payment. In fact very few male prisoners made use of the brothel. The great majority of prisoners were not fit enough to care about sexual intercourse. A good many of the rest shunned the brothels on moral grounds and others were homosexual. There was also a political risk in going to the brothel. A man might go there and lie with a woman, who unknown to him, was a favourite of an influential prisoner. A few days later he would mysteriously disappear.

Several times in these few days my friends emphasised to me how important it was not to offend any of the prisoner hierarchy. Since the lower levels of the hierarchy ramified down to the hundreds of pimps, hangers-on and trusties who were given the soft jobs around the block leader's premises, and since thousands of prisoners were ready to pass on information to these in return for extra food or protection, this virtually meant that you must not offend anybody at all. If one could keep oneself to oneself, and attract no notice, the camp need not be such a terrible place. The main thing was to keep quiet, and, as far as possible, conform.

It was the middle of January 1944, when I was due to report for my first labour commando. But the day before I had to go I fell sick. I had felt very weak ever since I came to the camp. Now I began to sweat and feel feverish, and in a few hours I hardly knew where I was. I have a vague recollection of lying ill in the block, of a doctor coming to see me, and of being carried to the camp infirmary. For a time I was delirious with pneumonia. This left me very weak and I was considered quite unfit to work for the time being. I was discharged from the hospital but instructed not to return to my block. I was to report to another section of the camp, known as the little camp, until I had recovered.

The little camp was separate from the main camp, but was still within the electric fence which surrounded the whole place. Only the unfit lived here; those who were going to die and for whom it was not worth doing anything; those who were chronically unfit; and the convalescent.

When I entered my new block, which held about a thousand men, I was horrified. Living conditions in the big camp were certainly tough, but compared with those in the little camp they were not at all bad. Here the bunks were designed to hold not two men but ten, sleeping head to foot. In fact most of them held twelve or thirteen. The filth and stench were indescribable, for the prevalent disease was dysentery, and most of the men were too weak to move from their bunks. There they lay, stained and spattered with vomit and excrement, dying and waiting to die.

For the first few days I was still so weak that I had no choice but to lie helpless in one of these filthy bunks. We were so closely packed that when one of us turned, everybody else had to move. Next to me, I remember, was a Russian. He was suffering from tuberculosis, and every now and again he coughed up phlegm. He was so weak, poor fellow, that all he could do was to spit it into an empty jam tin which he kept near his head. One morning I awoke with a strange sensation in my nose. He had upset his spittoon and I was lying with my nose and mouth in a pool of phlegm. I remember thinking quite clearly to myself that I could not possibly survive in those conditions, that I had probably two or three weeks to live. I became even more convinced of this a few days later when the poor fellow died and was carried off.

How I survived those few weeks I cannot imagine. Some of the inmates who were not so ill brought me scraps of food, and I had been given some pills at the infirmary; but I must nevertheless have been extraordinarily lucky. As soon as I had the strength to get out of the bunk I did so. For the rest of my six-month stay in the little camp I slept on the floor.

Once I had become accustomed to the stench and the filth and the wretched food of the little camp, I realised that there were many advantages in being there. The sick were spared the terrible physical risk of working in the quarry or on the railway, and the gruelling ordeal of the Appel. Because they were largely given up for dead they were outside camp politics with all its dangers. They were not hounded, nor were they involved in the mad rush which began at four o'clock every morning in the main camp and did not end until after the Appel. All this made life in the little camp comparatively peaceful.

There was also time to use the ablutions and lavatory facilities. These were concentrated in a building in the middle of the little camp. Along one side of it were fountains similar to those in the blocks in the big camp. Along the other side were the lavatories, or, I should say, *the* lavatory. It was most spectacular. It consisted of a continuous deep trench about eight feet deep and eight feet across, and about twenty yards long. A low wall about fifteen inches in height ran along the edge of the trench, and a long wooden spar ran parallel to it, a little higher, and farther back from the edge of the trench. To use the lavatory you squatted on the wall and leaned back so that the spar supported you in the small of the back. At regular frequent intervals the pit was drained off.

The arrangement was efficient and sanitary, but it was a sinister place. If prisoners wished to pick a fight with each other, or if the Kapos wanted to liquidate anyone, the lavatory pit was usually the place chosen to do it. And if the camp hierarchy had to dispose secretly of the corpse of a man who had met his death in some other part of the main camp, they usually chose the invalids' lavatory pit at a time when there were no S.S. around to see.

I had been in the little camp for five or six weeks when my younger brother, Charles, arrived at Buchenwald. I had heard from my parents while I was at Fresnes prison that he had joined the Resistance and had later been captured by the Germans. Like me, he had gone to Fresnes. After a journey of several days in one of those tragically overcrowded transports (two hundred men to a wagon) which often ended in death for considerable numbers of people, he had arrived at Buchenwald. He had been too ill to be considered for work, and was sent straight to the infirmary. Now here he was, sent to the little camp to convalesce— or die.

He had been put in another block not far from mine, and a

man who knew us both sent word to me that he was there. As soon as I could walk steadily I went to his block. It was a curious reunion. We were both glad to see each other alive and overjoyed to be reunited. Yet we were each, without saying it, shaken to see how weak the other had become, and depressed to find the other in the same hopeless predicament. We each wondered how long the other could last.

For some weeks my brother was so ill that I had no time to think about myself. I did what I could for him, using my extra experience of the camp and extra strength to scrounge food for him from my friends. Gradually he got back to the state of health which in the camp passed for normal.

Conditions in the little camp were so bad that when a prisoner felt well enough, his inclination was to get back to the main camp. I suggested this to my brother as soon as he seemed as fit as he was likely to become, but he was most unwilling. He took the view that if we returned to the big camp we should have to work and that if we worked we would be assisting the German war effort. He said that he had no intention of doing this if he could possibly help it.

I felt sympathetic towards this point of view, of course. Also I had heard and seen enough in the little camp to be apprehensive about the risks of joining the labour commandos. Men had been brought back to camp, crushed and broken by the loads of stone they had been compelled to carry from the quarry. I had seen the bodies of men who had collapsed under the weight of railway sleepers. There were other forms of work which were not so arduous, but to be assigned to these depended on patronage from friendly Kapos or on sheer good luck. I knew that neither I nor my brother were strong enough to survive a labour gang. All in all, therefore, I agreed with Charles that it would be better to stay in the little camp. We were in the fortunate position of being just about fit enough to survive in those unpleasant and insanitary surroundings, but weak enough not to attract the attention of some unsympathetic labour Kapo who might send us back to the commandos. We stayed on.

In such a place one naturally saw the best as well as the worst in human nature. One day my brother came to take me over to his block, saying:

'There is a man I want you to meet. He nursed me when I first got here and I thought I was going to die. He is a saint.'

I still recall my sense of revulsion when I saw M. He was a stage caricature of the most effeminate type of homosexual. His walk, his figure, his manner were all unbelievably grotesque. He was of more than medium height and not badly built, but his mincing gait and gestures made him look smaller and slighter. He might have been any age between thirty and fifty. His face was womanish without being in the least attractive. It was broad, squat and Asiatic, with empty, characterless eyes. The only feature about him that did not repel was his voice, which was that of a very cultivated man. He came from an ancient Rumanian family, and had been educated well and expensively in France. He had been a horticulturist and had specialised in roses. He was a sincere and profound Roman Catholic. Now, in the little camp, he had shown where his true genius lay. It was to care more for the most wretched and degraded sick human beings than for himself. Month after month he fetched and carried water, medicine, food or bowls of soup; or he would sit and hold a dying man's hand while he gasped out his final prayers. He became one of the legends of Buchenwald in his own lifetime. He saved many lives, including my brother's, by his ministrations. And although he lived in the deepest of filth and disease for more than two years, he survived.

I had by now spent quite a long time in the little camp and I had come to the conclusion that we must leave it and get ourselves assigned to some work in the big camp. For my apprehensions had been aroused by a number of things. On the Eastern front the German casualties were enormous. The medical services were short of blood plasma, and the prisoners of war were being asked to volunteer blood. Camp prisoners who were in the labour commandos were not asked, however, for their labour was urgently required and they must be kept as fit as possible. Every prisoner who contributed a pint of blood was promised a sausage. At this stage rations were being drastically reduced and many prisoners offered their blood for the extra food. The sausage was not enough, of course, to counteract the effect of losing a pint of blood, and as a result large numbers of the donors died. But many prisoners could not resist the temptation, even though they knew what a risk they were taking. Many a Russian, Pole or Frenchman virtually committed suicide for the sake of a single ersatz sausage.

The second thing which I noticed was that, from time to time, invalids with apparently good prospects of recovery were moved from the little camp to the hospital area and never returned. There was a block, isolated from the rest of the camp, which was officially known as the Clinical Department of the Waffen S.S. Institute of Hygiene. It was here, I believe, that during the early years of the war human experiments, mainly to produce remedies and inoculations, were carried out on criminals and Jews. Later on the Germans experimented on other kinds of prisoners. Men between the ages of eighteen and forty-five, the age of the serving soldier, were in particular demand as guinea pigs. To begin with a guinea pig received certain privileges, such as good beds, good food, which included white bread, and milk. It was a tempting proposition—but a dangerous one, as so very few came back.

It was now also becoming evident that being in the little camp was no longer a protection against work. Indeed for heavy work with a high casualty rate invalid labour, which was expendable, might even be preferred. I remember that one day a Kapo from the big camp appeared in the little camp and formed a squad of the least unfit of us to go and work on the railway. The squad returned that night minus several of its original members, who had collapsed under the weight of the rails they were forced to carry. My turn would undoubtedly come. With lung trouble and an unsound leg, I would be one of the first to collapse. I decided that to remain in the little camp was simply to wait for the inevitable end.

I tried to persuade Charles that we must get back to the big camp and get regular work.

'I have told you,' he said. 'I don't intend to do a thing for these people. It is a betrayal of my country.'

'If you stay here,' I said, 'you will not be able to help France or yourself. Back in the big camp we may have a chance. Here we do not.'

Charles was much more sanguine by temperament than I. Because things in the little camp were going reasonably well at the time, he saw no danger. I had to talk to him for several days before I could convince him that I was right. Finally he agreed to come with me.

So I went to one of T.'s underlings and said that my brother and I were now recovered from our illnesses and wanted to work. The next day he came with a chit which authorised us to return to the main camp. That evening we reported to the Kapo of Block 26, which contained about five hundred prisoners.

7

After a respite of several months the high-speed routine of the big camp was extremely exhausting. It was a little less intolerable to be awakened at four a.m. in summer than at four a.m. in winter, but there was the same mad rush and the same sense of utter confusion. I was warned that it was now unsafe to take off one's clothes to go to sleep, for they would almost certainly be stolen. So for the remainder of my time in the camp, I slept in my clothes with my head pillowed on my shoes.

My brother was assigned to factory work outside the camp and I was sent to join a squad of men whose job was to clean up a grove of trees located just inside the camp limits. The work, which consisted mainly of digging down deep enough to uncover the roots of trees which had been felled, was not unduly arduous for men who were reasonably fit. But for us it was very hard indeed. I was exhausted by the time we broke off at lunchtime to eat our round of bread. All through the afternoon I wondered how long I could stand it. And after roll-call that night all I could do was collapse on my bunk. I was unable even to bother about food.

The next weeks were tough. I remember one incident. An old Russian, a member of our gang, obviously found the work far too much for him. The S.S. in charge went to him and said, not unkindly: 'Fed up, eh? Not worth living?' The old man nodded. The S.S. turned and told a prisoner to fetch a rope. When he returned with it he was ordered to make a noose, put it round the old man's neck and hang him. This was done. Was it sadism on the part of the S.S.? Or was it, on the contrary, a kind of humane wish to put a creature out of its misery?

My morale would have sunk very low if it had not been for my fellow-prisoner Richard, whom I met at this time. Richard was one of the many heroes of Buchenwald. An engineer by profession, he was a slim man of about forty, whose hair was already turning grey. He had a fine aristocratic face, a beautiful brow and a keen, straight nose. He had a peculiar and very attractive way of speaking, with the slow and careful pronunciation of a Burgundian. But his most outstanding feature were his shrewd, kindly, blue eyes. His penetrating look was always sympathetic and humorous, but never critical. You felt that he knew everything about you, what you had done, what you could and would do, and that you could have no secrets from him. That I think was the key to his remarkable authority. We all went to him when we were in difficulties; although as often as not he had already appeared, as though by magic, at the right time and the right place.

On my back at the end of the day, I would sometimes turn my face despairingly to the wall and feel the last dregs of the will to live slipping out of me. As though by some miraculous gift of telepathy, Richard would guess my state of mind and appear beside me. He would make some silly joke, which would somehow make one respond.

'Now come on, old boy,' he would say. 'You're not going to let what happened today get you down? Not after what you did at Fresnes? And at Neue Bremm? You're not going to let *this* get you down after sticking all that?'

Then he would go on to tell some anecdote or joke, usually about himself, in which he made himself look a fool.

Often I stood on parade waiting for the Appel, with all my resources gone. At these moments I was on the point of deliberately collapsing on to the ground to let the S.S. haul me to the experiments block or finish me off with a pistol there and then. Suddenly I would feel a gentle dig in the ribs. Richard would be there, smiling, and he would start whispering some ridiculous story which even at that stage would make one smile.

He was the soul of generosity. Many times I saw him give his only piece of bread to a fellow-prisoner.

'I eat too well here,' he used to say. 'I need to cut down.' He lived at the edge of starvation to succour others. His moral and physical bravery was phenomenal. He was always ready to die so that others could live.

After a few weeks in the wood I collapsed and had to be carried back to the little camp. There was no choice in the matter this time. I remained there for about four weeks. I was still anxious to get out. As soon as I began to feel fit again, I asked one of T.'s underlings if some alternative work could be found. He said he would do what he could. When I returned to Block 26 I was told that I had been assigned to work with a commando which was building new barracks a couple of miles along the road connecting the camp with the main road to Weimar.

This work, which we had to march to, was quite tolerable for some months. My squad was engaged in laying the foundations of these buildings and constructing what I imagine were to be the cellars, air-raid shelters and ground floors. Our main activity was carrying bricks on carriers made like stretchers, a man at either end. The Kapo of the commando was a fine character, a Jehovah's Witness, who was just and humane to his squad. When the S.S. men turned their backs, as they frequently did, we were allowed to work at our own pace. Unfortunately he was replaced after a couple of months by another Kapo, who was much less agreeable. In order to stand well with the camp hierarchy, he kept non-Germans and non-communists hard at work. By now, however, some of us have discovered that it was possible to swing the lead from time to time. These buildings were going to be very large. The foundations were deep, the cellars tortuous. If one timed one's disappearance and reappearance carefully, one could drop down into an underground corridor, or curl up in a cellar, and take it easy for an hour or two. My brother (who had now joined me) and I spent several hours lying in these hideouts, talking or taking a nap. Since nearly two hundred men were working on the site, the absence of two or three individuals was never noticed.

I had more energy and health at this time than I ever had again in the camp. I never went to the cinema, but I did use some of my spare time in a civilised way. I had always tried to keep a diary, and now I continued it much more systematically, writing in a small hand on thin sheets of notebook paper scrounged from the canteen. (Somehow I managed to preserve these, and still have the originals.) Once or twice I went to concerts. These concerts, which the S.S. tolerated and even encouraged, illustrate one of the many contradictions of Buchenwald. When they were official they took place in the central hall, the one which was used at other times as an assembly position for those who had been chosen for the worst and very often fatal transports.

There were also unofficial concerts where the musical standard was even higher. These took place underground, and were arranged for members of the prisoner *élite* of the camp. The only time I was invited to one of these was to a most memorable trio, which included a fellow prisoner, the famous French violinist, Marcel Hewitt. In fact, there was a great deal of talent in the camp—Russian singers, dancers, a leading clown, a gypsy with a performing bear, and many others.

The S.S. were not so tolerant, however, about religion, which was officially banned. A few extreme sects, like the Jehovah's Witnesses, were quite open about their religion—indeed it was because of their religion they were in the camp at all. They were regarded by both S.S. and communists as being in a special, somewhat eccentric, comparatively harmless category of their own. They did not obtrude upon the general attention, and their reputation for fearlessness and readiness for martyrdom was well known. They would have died rather than disavow their faith. For these reasons, therefore, the S.S. left them alone.

It was different with the Roman Catholics. As soon as Roman Catholics came into the camp and prayed publicly they were approached by their more experienced fellow prisoners and advised to be discreet. They were warned that even if the S.S. did not get to know of these public activities, the communists would, and that serious trouble would result. But religion was practised secretly. Jan Robert, a young Dutchman, a man of great courage and charm, worked in a labour gang which somehow had managed to make contact with Roman Catholic priests in Weimar. Through them holy bread was smuggled into the camp and conveyed to Robert. He in turn distributed it to trusted friends who could hand it out to those who wanted it.

I was one of these. A friend of mine obtained some leather from the leather shop, and another some thread from the shoemakers. With this I made a little bag to hold the host. For the remainder of my time in the camp I distributed holy bread when the occasion demanded it to fellow Roman Catholics, who could be trusted not to talk about it. If a man's need for it was very great, I would give him a piece of the host, which he would then consume at a private celebration of his own.

The very fact of being a Roman Catholic, with its right-wing political associations in many countries, created a danger for those prisoners who had incurred a breath of suspicion in the communist camp hierarchy. When I first arrived at the camp there were a number of known Roman Catholic priests, but these were soon afterwards rounded up and sent to Dachau, where they remained until the end of the war. A few, who had concealed the fact that they were priests, managed to stay in Buchenwald.

I met very few Jews at Buchenwald. They came and went, staying only a short time on their terrible way to one of the murder camps. The small number that remained for any appreciable time were orthodox Jews from countries like Poland and Rumania. They were solemn, dignified, bearded men who tried to practise their religion and read their books, meeting in small, secret, whispering groups between the huts. Few of us were able to compare in faith and fortitude with them. They were quiet and humble, and created no problems for their gaolers or their fellow prisoners. Whenever they were put to the test, they showed utter fearlessness and integrity. But I doubt if any of them survived to the end of the war.

Amongst the many Russians in the camp there was a contingent of about two hundred officers and other ranks. That they were in the camp at all was against the laws of war. They had been captured in ordinary warfare and should have been treated as normal prisoners of war, with all the safeguards and accepted international standards that such prisoners are entitled to.

These Russians always behaved splendidly. Each man not only made the best of himself, his manner and his appearance as an individual, but he also continued to regard himself and to conduct himself as part of a military unit. They all looked and walked like soldiers. Their *esprit de corps* was magnificent. There were two senior officers among them, who behaved just as though they were in command of a brigade of Guards. Whenever these Russians appeared in public, whenever they emerged from the block to Appel or to the cinema, they marched in formation with one of their senior officers at their head.

One day we heard that the Russians had done something to offend the S.S. and that in consequence they were to be punished for breach of discipline. They were to be deprived of rations for two days. This was a very severe sentence in view of the meagre state of our rations at the time. In Block 26 we decided that to make sure that the Russians did not starve to death, we must share our rations with them. I was one of the two men deputed to carry the food to the Russians. It consisted of only about a slice of camp bread per day per man, so we had no difficulty in carrying it in a hamper.

Word was sent ahead to the Russians that we were on our way. When we reached their blockhouse we found that they were all drawn up in full military formation on the edge of the square. Their senior officers were at their head. One of them marched forward to meet us, and as he saluted us, the whole formation of half-starving men sprang to attention. The senior officer then made a short, formal speech of thanks which was translated for us by another officer. A small party marched forward to take the basket from us as if receiving regimental colours at a church parade, and resumed its position. At another command the squad marched back to its block. One is inclined to mock at rigid discipline when things are going well, but in those desperate days this feat of discipline was most impressive.

Feats of indiscipline could be equally inspiring. One day a group of American soldiers, who should never have been sent to a concentration camp at all, arrived at Buchenwald. On their first day they refused to attend the roll-call, as a protest against the food. Being deprived of their relatively high standard of living gave them a kind of daring that we could only marvel at. When the whistle for the Appel was blown they sat on the floor of their huts and refused to move. Even when the S.S. came and beat them up with sticks they refused to go out. Taken by surprise, the S.S. decided that they had better make the roll-call with these men still sitting down.

The Americans suffered terrible reprisals for this during the ensuing few days, and I doubt whether any of them left the camp alive. But how their fine example fired us and raised our morale! And how foolish and futile the S.S. brutes had looked, if only for a moment or two. It was all too easy for an insidious feeling to grow inside one that one was in fact an inferior, worthless animal, who did not deserve to live; and that the S.S. were somehow superior in every sense and deserved to have the power they used. Now and again, thanks to the Russians and the Americans, the window of reality was thrown open for a moment, and through it came air and light, which enabled one to carry on and renewed our hope and faith.

There were several thousand other Russians in the camp, but they were in a different category. They were Asiatic Russians, mainly other ranks, wartime troops with little training and little sense of discipline. There were also several thousand Poles. Except for seeing them *en masse* at the Appel, and meeting them occasionally in labour commandos, I made little or no contact with them. Indeed, it is amazing to look back and realise how little of Buchenwald a prisoner might see in several months. The rush of the daily routine, the narrow environment of the blockhouse, and above all the incredible fatigue, dulled one's observation. One was continually tired, drained of both physical and mental energy. Often it seemed almost impossible to carry on. I suppose that in a paradoxical way it was being so exhausted that enabled one to survive.

For some months there were a number of children in the camp, all very young, between perhaps the ages of three and ten. They were the offspring of prisoners who had been killed by accident, who had died of disease in the camp, or who had been deliberately destroyed by the Germans for leading local resistance. A few of the children came to Buchenwald from Auschwitz, where their parents had gone to the gas chamber. In many cases, neighbours had adopted one or more of these tiny orphans, and when they in their turn were taken to a camp they had had no choice but to take the children with them. Some of the babies had even been born in a camp.

They now had the run of the place. Many of the Kapos and leading members of the prisoner hierarchy were quite fond of the children and made pets of them. They gave them extra food and dressed them in good clothes. I remember one little boy who was beautifully dressed in a well-cut coat and charming little knee-boots. There was another little boy of six or seven, who could go where he liked and do what he chose. He would push open the door of a block, or run into the kitchens and grab a piece of bread, and nobody tried to stop him.

They were only in Buchenwald a short time. One day one of the eldest of them found a prisoner who he said had betrayed his parents to the Gestapo. The lad started stoning the wretched creature and the other children copied him. As the noise increased, adult prisoners approached to see what was happening and joined in the stoning themselves. In this brutal way their victim was soon disposed of and the parents of the children were supposedly revenged. Shortly after this horrible episode the children left the camp. I was glad to see them go. There was something terrible about them.

I did not witness this stoning myself. But there were two or three other occasions when I did see assassinations. If a prisoner for some reason or other upset his neighbours, usually by stealing their food, he might be stoned or kicked to death. I was walking between two blocks one summer's evening, when suddenly the door burst open and a man rushed out. Before he had gone ten yards a horde had poured out after him. They caught him and began to kick him. When he was incapable of moving they collected stones and threw them at him. He was dead in a few minutes. He had been accused of betraying a colleague to the S.S.

This kind of thing was done out of sight of the S.S. The S.S. were concerned only with breaches of discipline and with disposing of prisoners who had collapsed and for whom it was not worth while, from their point of view, trying to do something. From time to time they flogged prisoners, and now and again they hanged one or two. It was quite possible to be in Buchenwald for several months, as I was, and see no signs of mass slaughter whatsoever. Now and again one saw a lorry load of corpses going to the crematorium, but they could have been the victims of disease, or the result of unsuccessful experiments; or they might have been sick prisoners who had collapsed after a particularly hard day in the quarry followed by a long and freezing Appel. In this case the S.S. might have finished them off with a hypodermic syringe at the infirmary.

The black market in the camp was a thriving business. The system was quite simple. Leading prisoners robbed the dead and dying of valuable things like furs, gold and watches, and exchanged them in the canteen for a wide range of articles—even champagne. These articles, or course, were supplied to the canteen from outside with the connivance of the S.S., into whose hands the gold and furs eventually passed.

Again, prisoners working in the tailoring or shoemaking commandos, when asked to make a uniform for the S.S., would draw far more material than was required, make an extra garment or an extra pair of shoes, and sell this in the camp at fantastic price. Anybody who could pay the prices could get hold of a good knife if he wanted one. Some of the men in my block had sets of tools. For the gift of a few cigarettes I had received in a Red Cross parcel a Russian in my hut made me several articles, including a cigarette-holder with my number engraved on it and the head of a madonna, carved from the wood of Goethe's oak.

8

The task of selecting the men who were to go on each transport was carried out by the chief of the Arbeitstatistik. In other words by T. He and his lieutenants almost invariably knew which transports were relatively comfortable and which were fatal. Broadly speaking, they would send prisoners they approved of on the good transports and prisoners they disapproved of on the bad ones. To be fair to them, this did not mean that they always put communists on the good ones and non-communists on the bad. The top priority for bad transports were those prisoners who caused the most trouble in the camp, and who made their lives as camp leaders more difficult for them. Occasionally, but only occasionally, they did not themselves know whether a new type of transport which had been requisitioned for some new destination would be good or bad.

Some transports took the prisoners to conditions which were far more agreeable than those of the camp. Others took them to conditions which were virtually lethal. The forest transports, for example, were almost like holidays. But the Dora transports for work on underground factory building were death sentences. The draftees were sent to work deep below the ground. Many never came up again. A Frenchman who went on a Dora transport might last for three months if he was lucky. A Russian, who was on the whole tougher and more used to manual labour, might last six months. The prisoners worked like slaves, drilling and hauling in filth and dust, sleeping and eating in the bowels of the earth without access to fresh air. They were never brought to the surface until the whole job was finished.

The notorious N.N. transports were in a class of their own. N.N. stood for *Nacht und Nebel*, or night and fog, which was the code name given to this type of transport in Berlin. The names of the men who were to be sent on any N.N. transport were drawn up not in the camp but at S.S. headquarters in Berlin. A complete list of nominees would be received at Buchenwald. In the case of all other transports only a figure for the total number of men required came to the camp from Berlin, and it was left to T. and his staff to select the names.

No one in the camp would know where an N.N. draft was destined for, but there was clear evidence by now of how little chance anyone had of surviving one. An S.S. guard would arrive from ouside the camp to take charge. Everyone on the N.N. list had to report to them wearing only the basic clothing issue of the camp. After a few months in the camp nearly everyone managed to scrape up a few extra articles of clothing or footwear, usually from friends who had died—an old flying jacket, a greatcoat or sometimes a pair of leather boots. Obviously little value was attached to the draftee's life, if he was to be deliberately stripped of the few extras which frequently stood between him and death from exposure. A man embarking on an N.N. transport was not liquidated, executed or otherwise deliberately done to death. He just disappeared without trace into the night and fog.

My first thought on hearing that my name was down for an N.N. transport was that I must have done something to offend the prisoner hierarchy, and that they were getting rid of me by sending me on a draft. But my friends assured me that, since the names came straight from Berlin, there could be no question of this. I now realise that it was far more probable that, after Hitler had agreed for political reasons that I was not to be executed formally as a prisoner of the state, the word had gone down to the S.S. that there was no reason why I should not be disposed of, in a discreet way.

The following day I saw the powerful Eugene Kogon, who had, as I have said, interceded with T. on my account.

Kogon was a quiet, dark, sympathetic-looking man. He knew all about my case and said that he would try to help me, although he made it clear that he also had many obligations to other prisoners. Everything had to be done on the basis of what the communists in the camp considered to be in their best interest. Personal considerations and feelings, though real enough, had to come second. He advised me to report sick and return to the little camp for the time being. He would declare me unfit for work and sign a chit to that effect. He hoped that this would save me from the transport. That was all he could do.

I went straight to the little camp.

After a day or two some friends came with the bad news that the N.N. transport had been held up. I would have to lie low for longer than we had bargained for. When the list of nominees for the transport had arrived from Berlin at the Arbeitstatistik headquarters, the prisoners working there as clerks had seen that a number of prominent camp communists were on it. Somehow these names had to be fiddled off the list and others substituted, all with explanations which would satisfy the S.S. authorities in Berlin. This would take some days to effect. So the word was passed through the camp underground that everything was to be done to delay the mustering and despatch of the N.N.

The next piece of news was that my brother was ill. He had developed a painful swelling of the jaw and throat and was in the infirmary. The doctors were treating him, but without success. There was a possibility that it was mastoid trouble, which would require a serious operation, at which anything could happen. The idea of leaving my brother in Buchenwald with that risk facing him worried me as much as the prospect of N.N.

Two or three weeks went by and then a third development added to my fears. Red Cross parcels and letters from home, which had been coming through to me fairly regularly, suddenly stopped. I drew only one conclusion from this. The camp underground must regard my chances of escaping the N.N. as hopeless.

I understood how they felt. It was not unkindness or cruelty or selfishness on their part. It was simply that what little power they had to keep alive had better be redirected to somebody who was going to live, not wasted on me. But although I understood, I did not feel any happier.

My diary at this stage is a curious mixture of profound pessimism about my fate and of interest in quite trivial things. My morale had sunk very low. Here and there in the pages there is a prayer, obviously composed in the conviction that I would be included in the transport and would perish within a few days of leaving the camp. Here and there are notes on things which I could not possibly have expected to be interested in again: reflections on a marriage between friends which my father had mentioned in a letter, and reflections on plans for refurnishing a part of our house which my mother had told me about.

There came a ray of light when I heard that Charles was better. His swelling had subsided and there would be no operation. He was up and about, but would have to visit the hospital regularly. He had been passed unfit for work indefinitely. Kogon had interested himself in his case and had personally certified that he was not for the time being to return to a commando. I was further cheered to hear that Charles's name was not on the N.N. list.

For the next six or seven weeks I remember very little. A day or two after hearing the good news about Charles I became feverish. When I recovered sufficiently to take any interest in what was going on around me I heard that the N.N. had been postponed again. There had been so many 'difficulties' in organising it that orders had come through from Berlin to postpone the transport.

I was still recovering from my fever in the little camp when I came to know a doctor called Dupont. He was a small man in his late twenties, with a strong, open face and most kind eyes. One of my closest friends at that time suffered from epileptic fits, from which he saved himself by taking special pills. Few of us knew of his disability. I doubt if anybody other than members of his family know of it today. Up to this time at the camp he had managed to retain a supply of these pills, but now his supply was running out. We all knew that if he were found by the S.S. in a fit, he would be despatched to the crematorium at once.

Dupont, who had worked in the underground and was well respected by the communists, had been posted to the hospital block. He was a very able doctor and had a number of contacts among the German medical staff working in the S.S. hospital. From these he discovered in time where this kind of pill was kept and somehow he got access to the key of the particular cupboard.

At the first opportunity he seized his chance to take some of the pills. The next day he came to our hut with a quiet, triumphant smile on his face. Dupont did not know my friend and he hardly knew me. He had everything to risk and nothing to gain from this kind act.

Dupont was a very reticent man. He wanted to retain his post in the camp, not only to preserve his own life, but also because he felt he had a duty to help the camp underground so far as he was able. His semi-privileged position was much coveted and there were plenty of people ready to move him out of it and usurp it, if they could. Moreover, he had come to the camp possessed of a great deal of recent information about the external underground. If any of his knowledge were overheard and passed on to the S.S., he would be re-interrogated. Or he might be reported to one of the communist bosses. For these reasons he kept very quiet, and on one or two occasions on which I drifted into talk about the French resistance movement, I found him positively evasive. But when I went to him, as I did several times, for some kind of medicine for myself or my friends he would say nothing, ask no questions and return some time later, again without a word and with a shy half-smile on his face. He would just open his hand and there the elixir would be.

We had need of these moral giants to keep us going. In my own experience our morale and will to live were never undermined by what the S.S. or the criminal and degenerate elements in the camp did. It was when we saw our own kind and our own friends behaving badly that the will to live sank lowest. When we let each other down all kinds of disruptive emotions were released, which added to our exhaustion and diminished the will to live.

At these moments the beast in us had its opportunity. Despair produced anger; anger led to aggression, and aggression to guilt; and guilt took us down to yet a lower rung of the ladder of desperation.

At a time when morale was low and we were extremely short of food, I was awoken one night by a curious noise. It was coming from underneath one of the tables in the centre of the block. I was relieved to find that it was only somebody eating and I went back to sleep. But the next day several of us found that our tiny reserves of bread had been stolen.

This had happened before. My brother and a few other young men had formed a kind of blockhouse police force to preserve discipline in general and to prevent thieving in particular. They made enquiries. Several people had heard the sounds of eating in the night. Though some of us were diplomatic, there was no concealing the identity of the culprit. He was a man who before the war was well known in public life in Paris.

The accused was 'tried' and found guilty. A very serious view was taken of his crime. Rations were down to their very lowest and men were dying of starvation. The thief was to be thrashed.

The thrashing was shocking. It was not so much what happened to the thief, but what happened in the process to my brother and the two or three decent young men who undertook to administer the thrashing. In losing their self-control, they seemed to behave no better than the S.S. They did not punish the thief; they very nearly killed him. It was not retribution; it was revenge.

I spoke angrily to my brother, telling him that he and his friends had behaved worse than the thief. I agreed that it was right to disgrace and punish the man; but he should have been forced to do extra work, give up part of his ration, or be sent to Coventry. In beating him up Charles and his friends had become animals who kick and kill because something deep, primitive and savage had taken control within them.

My brother tried to defend himself. The more he did so, the more my own anger rose. In a few minutes I, who had complained of his beating the thief, could almost have attacked and beaten him myself in a similar access of hate and fury.

These were the situations which exhausted and undermined us more than anything the Nazis or the privations of the camp could do. I turned away from my brother in a rage that was partly directed against him, partly against myself. I did not speak to him for many days; nor to anyone else. I lay sullenly in my bunk and gave up the will to live.

Many a brother would never have spoken to me again; but not Charles. When he heard that I was lying on my bunk refusing to see anyone, he sent me notes written on lavatory paper, begging me not to deprive him and his friends of my company. Day after day he wrote, causing me to reflect that the good and the bad lie very close in all of us and that this is the human condition with which we all must live. 'Forgive me and become yourself again,' he wrote, and in doing so he saved my life. In a few days I had recovered my equilibrium.

The next blow came with the dread news that N.N. was scheduled again. It was to leave very quickly. The camp grapevine was at work again. Within a few hours of the warning I had been informed that my name was still on it.

I went to see Kogon. He said he would do what he could, but he held out little hope. He could say I was sick, but the S.S., because I was named, would come and find me. He would be asked why he had sent me sick. However, he would see what could be done.

I made up my mind that, if Charles's name was on the list, I would go anyway. I would not be parted from him again. Otherwise I would try to escape. A few days later, walking in the camp, I found a four-leafed clover. It seemed to me a miraculous sign of good luck. I have kept it to this day.

The next day the camp Tannoy system blared out the names of about two hundred and fifty men who were on the N.N. list, and instructed them to report to the watch-tower. After having done so, we were told we could return to our blocks, but must be ready to report back to the tower and get into the trucks at instant notice. The moment had come. Again I was desperate.

For each category of prisoners in the camp one was elected to act as spokesman or representative. One of the spokesmen of the French in the camp was Captain T. R. I now went to him to beg his help in finding some way of avoiding the transport. He was obviously very embarrassed, but promised to think the matter over.

'You must understand that I am in a very difficult position,' he said.

I knew what he meant. He did not want to compromise his already shaky position with the communists by helping someone tarred, as he thought, with a right-wing brush. I left him without a word.

The next day I found myself by chance almost alone with Moriquand, a Frenchman who acted as interpreter for Jacob, the communist chief of the block, who spoke only German. I had never spoken to Moriquand before, but now we exchanged notes about our records. He was very distressed to hear that I was on this next N.N. and he said he would try to see if anything could be done to get me off it. I was used to these polite words by now. After all Moriquand had not known of my existence until we had met that day by chance.

I was very surprised, consequently, when an hour or two later, he sent another prisoner to take me to his room. The transport, he told me, would not leave Buchenwald that day at any rate. I was to meet him that night after the Appel.

'We are going to the Hospital Block,' he said, when we met later. 'A friend of mine may be able to help you.'

We walked into the Hospital Block quite freely. Moriquand obviously had considerable status here. With nobody accompanying us, we walked unchallenged down to one of the wards.

'My friend Rudolf is in charge here,' he said. 'And he has promised to help you.'

A strong, rugged man with red hair met us at the door. He stared keenly into my face with sharp, cunning eyes, as we were introduced.

'You can lie down here in a bunk, if you like,' he said. 'There is a fifty-fifty chance that nobody will notice you. The S.S. do not like coming over here for obvious reasons. The death-rate in this ward is the highest in the camp. In fact you will run a considerable risk of dying of disease yourself.'

'I am very grateful to you both,' I said. And that night I lay down happily among the dying.

The next day I received a message from Moriquand that N.N. was postponed again, but I had better remain where I was. I was very glad to do so. But now that my own immediate danger was temporarily removed, I began to worry about Moriquand and Rudolf. If the S.S. should chance to visit the ward and find me there the two of them would be done for. So that second night, before I lay down in the bunk, I went to see Rudolf in his office. I told him that I did not think I could stay any longer in his ward if it was putting him in danger.

'Danger?' said Rudolf. 'Le danger—c'est le parfum de la vie.' And he pushed me out of his room.

I saw a good deal of him in the next few weeks. He was a very remarkable man. With T., Kogon and a few others, he was one of the top leaders of the camp. In his youth, just after the First World War, he had been an anarchist. He had a national reputation as a communist and he had been in concentration camps ever since the early thirties. Years after he had last seen his wife and family he decided that, if he continued to keep their photographs and letters, he would weaken and break down. Nor must he write to them any longer. He must dehumanise himself, if he was to serve the cause effectively. Somehow he was able to put his family completely out of his mind for good. He was a fanatic with nerves of iron and a strength of will which was almost inhuman.

He made it quite clear to me that he proposed to help me only because he thought it might help the party. He was not unkind or unfriendly in manner—quite the reverse. But it was impossible to imagine that he was acting from any motives of Christian charity.

There was no sentiment about Rudolf. He was adept at assessing whether a patient would live or die, and if he was sure the patient would die, he would cheerfully hasten his end. He only helped those whom he thought would live. After all, his resources were limited, and it was wrong as well as impractical to try to help the 'losers'.

While I lay in my bunk in his block, several of his patients died. Rudolf would come along with a couple of orderlies and haul the bodies off without a qualm to the lorry, which would carry them to the crematorium. I remember lying there one day, feeling very weak, for my lung trouble had developed again, and realising that the prisoner a few feet away from me had died. In a few minutes Rudolf had come up, stripped the corpse, heaved it off the bed, its head thudding against the ground. I remember there was magnificent tatooing which stood out brilliantly on the livid chest.

Rudolf was one of the prisoner hierarchy who had considerable power of life and death. As the war went on and occupied territory expanded, more and more people had to be sent into the camps. From time to time therefore the S.S. would decide that in order to conserve rations and keep down numbers, another two hundred prisoners had to be liquidated.

Had I been stronger it might have occurred to me that Rudolf might think he had risked quite enough for such a weakling as I. He might have administered an injection which would speed my end. But Rudolf was a man of his word, and had promised to save my life. He and his orderlies did their best to nurse me back to health.

I had been with Rudolf about a week when he came in and told me that there had been yet another postponement of N.N. It was beginning to look as if it might never leave after all. Cheered as I was by this news, I was in low spirits for I was still really sick. My lung had not fully cleared up after my bout of pneumonia, and I lay weak and depressed in Room 8 for two or three weeks. Suddenly I was brought out of my depression with a terrible shock. I was awakened from a half-sleep by a chorus of camp loud-speakers. At first I thought it was a dream, but in a minute or two I knew it was real. N.N. was to leave in a few hours. As I lay there I could hear my number being blared out again and again. And what was more the S.S. knew I was missing from my block for I could hear that instructions were being given to the S.S. guards to find out where I was.

I was in a panic. Rudolf was unperturbed. He went about his business as though nothing had happened. It was not long before the S.S. had scrutinised the hospital lists and found my number was in Rudolf's ward. Two of them rushed across to the hospital and burst into Room 8. They stood over my bed, looking huge and brutal, and roaring with rage. I was to get up and report to the transport at once, sick or not sick, or I would be shot.

Two things saved me. My own fear and Rudolf's courage. I was so paralysed with fear that I could not have got up and walked. But in any case in a second or two Rudolf was on the scene. A curious thing about a certain type of German is that he always wants to howl at people, and is very much impressed by being howled back at. Rudolf, a German himself, simply stood and howled at the S.S.

'Can't you see, you fools, the man is dying. He'll be dead in two days. If you want to put a dead man on the truck, do it. Don't blame me for what happens to you, you bloody fools.'

The S.S. were so cowed by this counter-blast that they turned and left.

'That's the way to treat those idiots,' said Rudolf, coolly, as he returned to his work.

I felt better after this and even resumed making entries in my diary. The following day, Rudolf and I heard the camp loud-speakers announce that the N.N. transport would leave forth-with. A few outstanding names were reported, but there was no mention of mine. Later Rudolf came and told me N.N. had left.

I remained with Rudolf a few more days. By the time I left my lung was much better. Moreover, he had written out a chit for the Arbeitstatistik which stated that I was now fit for light work and should not be sent on any transport. It was the best thing that had happened to me in Buchenwald for many months. I left him feeling very grateful and much happier than when I had gone to Room 8 with Moriquand.

This was far from being the only occasion on which my life was saved by Rudolf. Indeed he never failed me. As I have said, he was not a man of sentiment and he certainly acted on the verdict which had been pronounced upon me by T. and the top communists. This verdict in short I owed to my father having been one of the few active French pre-war anti-fascists, to having myself been one of the earliest Resistants and oldest prisoners among the French, and also to the fact that I had never belonged —rare among members of my class and age-group—to any of the many fascist organisations which flourished in France before the war.

9

I returned to Block 26 in the big camp. Immediately I entered the block I heard that several of my best friends had left the camp on the N.N. transport. The feeling of elation at having escaped N.N. with which I left Room 8 now gave way to a feeling of deep depression mingled with guilt. I was tortured by the thought that I had been saved while others had gone to their fate.

My new labour commando was construction work on the sides of the road just outside the gates of the camp. The work was far from light. It consisted of wheeling barrowloads of brick and stone. I would find it beyond me today, when I am fit and well. Fed on those rations and living in those conditions, the strain was tremendous. The combination of impossibly hard work and this deep feeling of depression was almost more than I could bear.

There was, however, one improvement in the general situation. The camp was now so full and the S.S. had been so reduced in number because of the drain on German manpower, that discipline and supervision had become considerably relaxed. It was now possible, if you were reasonably discreet and on good terms with the prisoner medical staff, to get excused from work for short spells. You could spend a few days at a time in your block without reporting sick and being transferred to the little camp. Obvious and protracted malingering was not tolerated, but well-judged and reasonably justified work-dodging could be managed.

I was enjoying one of these 'confined to barracks with light duties' or 'Schoenungs', as the Germans called them, when I had another terrible fright. A friendly German who had contacts in the camp labour office came and told me that a transport was being arranged to leave Buchenwald for work at Dora, one of the worst transports. My name was on it. Once more I went to Rudolf.

Rudolf was very surprised that my name was down for any kind of transport, and insisted that there had been a clerical mistake which would be corrected in good time. He looked at my work chit again and read out the phrase which prescribed the work commando I was in and which stated that I was not eligible for a transport until further notice. I was all right, Rudolf said. He told me to go back to my block, carry on as before and ignore what I had been told. If by the merest chance my name *was* left on the Dora list and the mistake was not spotted, he would have no difficulty in getting it off. I left him feeling reassured.

But when I got back to Block 26 and discussed this development with two or three of my close friends, a question suddenly arose in our minds. How and why had my name got on the list in the first place? Who had put it there? The selection for the Dora transports, unlike the N.N., was made by T. and his men at the Arbeitstatistik. Whom had I offended? I went to my bunk that night but did not sleep.

The next day our spokesman, Captain T. R., on whom I had turned my back a few weeks previously when he refused to help me escape N.N., said he had something very grave that he wanted to talk to me about. He said that apparently it was being put about by some friends of mine that it was he who had been responsible for my name being put down for the Dora transport. This, he said, was completely untrue and he wanted me to know it.

I accepted his word. But it now occurred to me that the responsibility might lie with somebody else within the French detachment of prisoners. The French detachment, after all, was not composed entirely of ex-officers of the French Army who had fought with the Resistance. It was indeed a kind of microcosm of Buchenwald as a whole. It included regular soldiers, com-

munists, parliamentary politicians of right, left and centre, Paris
crooks, pimps and black marketeers, men of honour, desperadoes
and riff-raff. It was a collection of Frenchmen, who had nothing
in common except nationality. It occurred to me, especially since
I seemed to be on good terms with the German prisoners, that
my danger might be coming from the French.

Later on another leading member of the French group came to
see me. This was C., an influential communist. He told me that
as the chances of survival in the camp became more and more
slender, as it became more and more necessary for a man to know
who his real friends and his enemies were, it was essential for us
all to know what we stood for. He said that the French in the camp
were now rallying together on the platform of political commit-
ment to action in the post-war world on the basis of three prin-
ciples. These were complete loyalty to de Gaulle; total acceptance
of the Atlantic Charter; and liquidation of the huge industrial
and financial monopolies, which in France had formed a state
within a state. If I would promise to support this programme now
and after the war, in return the French in Buchenwald would do
their best to secure my survival in face of everything. We talked
for some time. I told him that I did not think in terms of political
programmes, but in terms of the two things that really mattered
to me, my country and my religion. For them I would spend my
last drop of blood and it was for them that I had done what I had
in the past. It was no use my pretending to anything more.

He seemed to find this entirely satisfactory, and said so. But I
was now seriously worried. After all, though we were all in daily
danger of death from disease or liquidation, the allies were gain-
ing ground in Europe and the end of the war in the Allies' favour
was thinkable, if not in sight. Just as there would be a struggle for
power in France and Germany between left, right and centre when
the war ended, so there would be a struggle for power in the
camp between the elements of each national contingent *now*.
Certainly the French communists, if they had any say in the
matter, would prefer to see a French Roman Catholic aristocrat
on the Dora list rather than one of their own members or sym-
pathisers. T., the German communist, might think more of me

than of some French black-marketeer. But if the leading French communists went to him and said that in post-war France the black-marketeer had promised to help them, whereas I was inevitably their enemy, would he, in the interests of the international communist brotherhood, have to comply?

I began to hate my fellow countrymen as a group almost more than I hated the S.S. In a sense more, because, as I have said, we saw so little of the S.S. anyway. There were a few noble and generous souls among the French, who were at Buchenwald for having served their country and fought for liberty, but the rest were swine. It so often happened that the swindlers, thieves and traitors were on top, and spoke and acted for all the French in camp. They managed everything from the distribution of Red Cross parcels and mail to the rigging of transport rolls, and did so only out of self-interest. How many of the fine workers for the Resistance movement were sent off to be trodden to death in a cattle truck, so that some pimp from a Paris night-club might live? At this time I wrote in my diary:

What an infamous régime. This shameful dictatorship! The dictatorship of all that is most sordid. What happens here is beyond imagination. Stupidity and savagery have attained undreamed of limits. There is nothing to be done but submit, and to continue to bear the weight of captivity. But what is the point of it all? When I look at those who surround me (happily I do not see them the greater part of the time), I am filled with shame and disgust, not only for them but for the Resistance to which these men profess to belong! If this is the Resistance, then I don't want it. At no price do I wish for a Resistance of blackguards, bullies and convicts.

At this time an event took place from which the morale of the S.S. never completely recovered. The camp was bombed by the allies. It was in fact a raid on Gustlof, the adjoining factory, and although about two hundred prisoners working there were killed and a thousand injured, such was the precision (and the accurate information of the allies) that very few bombs fell on the camp itself. One sent the huge stone eagle over the main gate crashing to the ground. The famous panel above the gate, representing a monk, a priest, and a Jew under escort of an S.S. guard, was blown to bits. Another bomb destroyed the Goethe Oak, the only tree remaining within the camp limits. Tradition had it that Goethe used to walk out from Weimar to meditate beneath this tree, and that were it ever to die, catastrophe would fall upon Germany. The S.S. were a prey in any case to super-stition, and this in itself would have been enough deeply to distress them. But a more personal tragedy had occurred. A bomb had fallen at each entrance of the bunker where their wives and children sheltered—and almost all had been wiped out.

For days the S.S. were seen wandering bewildered, stunned by their terrible loss. However, their brutality, when evoked, was as violent as ever. A Pole, who had tried to escape in the chaos, was caught. They did not bother about a gallows. They simply flung a rope over the wall near the main gate, put the noose around his neck and hauled the poor wretch off his feet. He was not hanged but strangled. He suffered terribly at the end of the rope for many minutes.

The general atmosphere of disorganisation and panic increased the severity of the prisoner bosses. A few days after the bombing, I learnt that F. had died very suddenly. F. was a fine man and a devout Roman Catholic, and he had made no secret of his dis-approval of communism. He had been going around the camp quite normally and had not been complaining about his health. A message had come to his block telling him to report to the infirmary. Twenty-four hours later his friends in his block were told that he had been found to be suffering from a disease, the nature of which was not made known, and that it had been impossible to save him. This was the official report, but his friends were certain that F. had done or said something which had antagonised one of the influential communists in the prisoner hierarchy, and that he had been murdered as a result.

Richard, also, who had done so much to sustain the morale of many of us, was an indirect victim of the bombing. His leg was badly injured and had to be amputated. Just before the liberation he died on one of those terrible transports by which the German sought to empty the camp before the advancing allies.

One morning I received a note which was signed Albert de N. Although the N's were distant relations of mine, I hardly knew Albert at all. I recalled him as a pleasant, elegant and well-mannered young man, whom I had met once or twice before the war. His note said that he had arrived in Buchenwald a few days previously and that he was in Block 43. Hearing from mutual acquaintances that I had been in the camp for some time, he was taking the liberty of writing to ask for my advice. The prisoners who were looking after him, he said, were now advising him to leave the block and get some fresh air and nourishment to rebuild his strength. He thought that in order to get a change of air he might go on one of the transports. What did I think?

Albert certainly had many lessons of the camp to learn. He still had no clue to the kind of life which was being lived around him. On another occasion he wrote to me to say that it had struck him that, if the men around him could organise prayers every night, they would all be the better for it. He had no idea that the very saying of prayers, if observed, would be reported to the S.S. or to the communist bosses, which would almost certainly lead to the death of those who said them.

I went to see him several times in his block and each time he would ask for my advice. What would I do in his position? If I spoke the truth, my advice would be that he should remain in Buchenwald. In fact I urged him not to risk going on a transport. I told him he was not really fit enough to leave. However, he ignored my advice and volunteered on the first transport that was available. A few weeks later he was dead.

Another anxiety was added to my burden. Transports were being organised at a rapid rate. I was safe with my chit, but my brother was not. In the ensuing few weeks Charles was listed on two or three transports. Fortunately, in each case we were able to plead successfully with Kogon and his friends to get him off. But the danger could recur.

With the beginning of the cold weather my lung began to give me trouble again. My temperature began to go up alarmingly. I collapsed with fever. I remember being carried on a stretcher across the parade ground to the hospital. A Russian communist medical attendant took my temperature at the door. I heard him say it was 100°F. He went off to look at somebody else. While I lay there, a Belgian doctor who was working in the camp infirmary came up and took my temperature also. He told me it was 104°F. He had begun to give instructions as to which ward I was to go to, when the Russian returned. He demanded to know what was going on and why I was being moved. There was an argument and the Russian medical orderly took my temperature again. When he maintained it was 100°F., the Belgian accepted it without further ado. He did not dare argue because the Russian was known to be influential in the camp underground and he was not. However, my illness gave me some respite from normal worries. I noted in my diary a few days later:

'The ideal life here is to be "off sick" all the time.'

1 January 1945 came round. Things were at their grimmest. Until now the officers, who constituted the best element in the French contingent in the camp, had more or less held together. But now the group was being torn into factions under the terrible pressure of the intrigues to avoid the transports. And those who believed that they would survive Buchenwald were thinking in terms of self-interest and power in post-war France.

But even more disturbing were reports of preparations being put in hand for yet another big N.N. transport. Within a day or two of first hearing these reports, one of my friends who had been working in the Arbeitstatistik learned that my name was included in the list. I discovered next that this was not an N.N. transport, but a new type with an unfamiliar code name, S.3. Several hundred men were to be drafted to it, but that was all that was known about it. Certain rumours said that it was a good transport, but nobody really knew.

For some days I lay in the sick-bay in an agony of indecision. Should I stay in the hospital as long as possible and risk the S.S. finding me as they did before and flinging me into the truck? Or should I summon my strength, get up and venture to see if I could persuade somebody to get my name off the list?

I decided to get up and go to my block. I went to B., one of the most influential and respected of the French officers, to see if he would do what he could to save me from the transport. I found that the atmosphere was tense with fear and intrigue. Within an hour of my speaking to him everybody in the French group seemed to know I had been to see him and was speculating on what I had said to him, on what I might have promised, or revealed, if he could get me off the transport.

The next time that the names for the S.3 were announced I was relieved to find that mine was not included. As usual the men who were to leave were assembled in the cinema. The transport left for its unknown destination without me. Three weeks later, having accomplished its mission of helping to construct an underground factory, it returned to the camp. That is to say that those who had survived the mission returned. Six or seven hundred had died at work under the ground. Several dozen had managed to survive until they got out of the vans which had brought them back to Buchenwald. They died somewhere between the gates of the camp and the blockhouses. Only about a hundred regained their blocks. Their accounts of what they had gone through, even at that stage in our experience, appalled us. S.3 was terrible—that was clear.

Two days later the camp grapevine reported that another S.3 transport was being organised and would leave within a few weeks. My name was once more on the list. So was my brother's.

This was my lowest moment in all my four years of imprisonment. Until now I had always tried to keep back any news from my parents that would increase their anxieties. Now, however, it seemed to me that Charles and I had come to within a few days of our end. Charles had been ill and was still weak, and I was certain he could not survive even a week of S.3. I had a slight chance of escaping S.3 because I still possessed the work chit which said I was not eligible for transports. But my brother had nothing. I decided that if he went on S.3, I would go too. It seemed to me, weighing it all up, that we had come to the end of our tether. I must now tell my parents the truth, otherwise there would be weeks, perhaps months, when they would hear nothing and conjecture everything. It would be terrible, useless and unnecessary agony for them. I made up my mind to try to compose myself and use these last few hours to write my parents a long and full letter which would as calmly and as reassuringly as possible prepare them for hearing that we had met our end.

'Ma chère petite maman,' I wrote on 9 January 1945. The letter is in front of me now.

I am writing to you at a time when the situation has become so tragic that there are certain things I must tell you. If this message reaches you one of these days, what joy that would give me.

It seems certain now that we are going to be sent out on a tough working-party. Charles will die if he does not get suitable medical attention immediately. He has got to do everything possible to escape this transport. If his name is called, and not mine, I shall try to take his place. Our life is in God's hands. God has helped us up to now. If He wishes to save us, He will save us. If we must die, let His will be done. If I have to go, I shall go bearing Christ in my heart and on my heart. I know that Charles's feelings are the same. I ask forgiveness from all those to whom I have done any harm, whatever it may have been. I would have wished to be buried later at Vellemont near you, but if God does not permit this last blessing, His will be done.

Dearest Maman, you mustn't cry. You know your son will be waiting for you in a better world. I haven't given up hope of finding you again on this earth, but I am certain God will bring us together again in heaven. So there is no need to cry, dearest Mother. Our life down here is very brief. For us, it will have been shorter than for others, but I have had so many joys, so much good luck in being near to you and Papa that life, I'm sure, couldn't have done more for me. Don't be sad on that account. I can't tell you how much I love you, both of you, and I don't want to talk about it for I should begin to weaken: I must be strong.

I have said my prayers all these years. I want you to remember me often when you say yours. When you pray, I shall be near you, whether it's in the chapel of the Holy Virgin (behind the high altar, I think) at Saint Francis Xavier, or to Sainte Clotilde in our little chapel, too often empty, at the house at Pargny, in the church at Pargny or at Paris, in the evening after a walk, at Grosbois, and certainly, finally, at Lourdes, in the grotto where I made a vow to make a pilgrimmage every year of my life if I returned.

Father, don't think that I set out to face this new trial in a spirit of defeat. You will be before me, I shall behold you, in the time of trial, and if I must suffer, your wonderful example will be before me. I have never been very brave under stress, alas. I hope that with God's help I shall not be too unworthy of you. My great fear, my great grief, my great anguish are for my dear little Charles with whom I have so often been at odds alas. He and I have often thought about Pargny and our past life. We have planned a mass of changes for the garden, and the house (especially for the entrance hall). Charles has described to me the apartment at 52 Avenue de Saxe and I have shared it with you, from here, not very successfully, but a little all the same.

I see you, Mother dear, in bed in the mornings with all those books and newspapers. The light coming from the window on your right. Near the bed you've got a little table on which there seems to be a funny adjustable lamp from number 113!!

And now beloved dear Papa, and my very own Mama, I must leave you for some time. We are going to find each other and never part again. Let us turn our hearts to God; if the way ahead is hard, Christ will be with us, to help us, and the Holy Virgin will remember our grief, our sadness, and bend down to you and to us. Be brave, then. I embrace you as I love you. Make the sign of the cross on my forehead, once again. I love you.

Pierre

As the day for the departure of S.3 approached I realised that I had done the right thing to leave the hospital. It had now become absolutely essential to work, if one was to escape a transport. Earlier it had been the other way round. But now workers were needed in the camp. The rations were so reduced that they could not be stretched to support even the moderately sick, and the best way of disposing of the sick was to send them off on a transport. Unfortunately, other prisoners had come to this conclusion too. Everybody seemed to be trying to find work.

The S.S. had realised what was going on and to a certain extent approved of it. It was in their interest for the able-bodied to stay, and the weaker ones to be sent off. In fact, when the final arrangements came to be made for the second S.3, the S.S. announced that on the day of its departure, all prisoners who did not have work permits were to parade after the Appel. These would go on S.3. Selection would not be by name, after all, but by whether you had a work chit or not. I was safe. Charles was not.

The day for S.3 came. I attended the morning Appel. As soon as it was over I gave my work chit, my coat and my number, to Charles. I told him to keep out of sight so far as he could. He must on no account return to the sick bay, which the S.S. might scour if they saw their S.3 contingent was below strength. He was to keep on the move and, if he met anybody, he was to pretend he had broken away from his commando to get treatment. If there was difficulty he could produce his chit. He might get a beating, but it would prevent him being sent on the transport.

Meanwhile, I marched off with my labour commando to work on the terrace. If there was a check up on work chits before S.3 left, I would say I seemed to have mislaid mine. My friends in the commando could identify me, obviously, and several of them could answer that I *had* a work chit. For me, too, being without it might have meant a beating, but Charles's life would be saved. As it happened, I was lucky. Though my heart was in my mouth, the S.S. never came near us. Charles was lucky too. He hung around the back of his block and saw nobody.

The second S.3 left. It was a particularly noteworthy one. Eighteen hundred men were on it. When it returned to the camp a few weeks later, eight hundred were already dead. Another two hundred and fifty died en route between the station and the camp. About two hundred and fifty more died within a few days of getting back to camp. About five hundred survived long enough for their subsequent deaths not to be attributable to that ghastly journey.

10

Looking back on those last three months in the camp I cannot understand how the will to live persisted in me. One was trying desperately to escape transport after transport only to remain in the camp and die a lingering death from disease or to be killed. More and more prisoners were collapsing at work. More and more were being taken to the hospital for liquidation by injection. More and more were being shot out of hand by the S.S.

There would have been greater incentive to live if comradeship and fellowship had remained as strong and vital as it had at Neue Bremm or, indeed, in the first months at Buchenwald. But that had gone, as my best friends had gone. By now the camp was a jungle. We had almost lost our respect for each other and for ourselves. We groped on day by day for life, half wishing to be dead. Often I awoke in the mornings to the sound of reveille and gravely pondered the pros and cons of lying there until in some form or another death came and put an end to my misery.

But the will to live *did* persist. And we studied the technique of continuing to live with a desperate concentration, developed perhaps more of the habit of four years than by a real desire not to die.

Discipline in the camp was much slacker. There were fewer S.S. to watch us. Those who were left were the older and less efficient ones, for the younger men had been sent to the front. These older men were on the whole more tolerant, but from time

to time they were worried by news about the war. A minor trans-
gression might inflame them and they would start using their
sticks. We had learned many tricks, like getting into the centre
of the squad when marching or on parade, because it was the men
on the outside who got beaten up. We found there was a trick of
running which made you look as if you were going flat out, when
in fact you were going at about half speed. More and more it was
becoming important, even at the risk of a beating from the S.S.,
not to expend the whole of your energy on the working site.
If you did and you happened to strike a long Appel on a freezing
night, you would collapse. And that would be the end.

A few days after the second S.3 had left my labour commando
was switched away from work on the terrace. Our Kapo was
instructed to parade us the next day for work on the railway.
We were to join other labour commandos in laying the lines at
the far end of the railway which connected Buchenwald with the
main line to Weimar.

The next morning at about six a.m., in pitch darkness, we
paraded at the camp end of the railway line and got into railway
trucks. The engine pulled us the seven or eight miles to the other
end of the line. We worked there till dark. Then we were pulled
back to the camp. This was by far the worst work that I had been
given to do and I knew that if I went on with it long enough it
would kill me. It consisted mainly of carrying lengths of rail from
stacks at the sides of the track up to the section of the line where
they were to be laid. In the first day I saw several men collapse
under the weight. That night we took several crippled men back
with us. Two or three were brought back dead.

The next two weeks were frightening. It so happened that the
little detachment I was working with was made up of short men.
I was by far the tallest. The weight always falls on the tallest man.
There was something ludicrous, mad, farcical about it. If I
hunched my shoulders and stooped a little to equalise the weight,
the S.S. hit me for slacking. If I straightened, I was carrying
enough weight for two. It was a mental nightmare as well as an
insufferable physical strain.

After fourteen days of this I decided that I must feign some kind of illness to get me off the railway commando right away. There were ways of provoking an artificial fever, like taking a good deal of aspirin and hitting one's arm against the wall until it was numb. Another well-tried method of producing symptoms of illness was to tie a piece of string or cloth tightly below the knee. Several hours later the ankle would swell and you could go to the doctor and say you had sprained it. This was always good for a few days' *Schoenung*.

I had never tried this trick before and I did not make a very good job of it. Or, rather, I made too good a job of it. I tied the cord before I went to bed. I woke a few hours later, in terrible pain, to find that my leg had turned almost black. I was appalled by its appearance and thought that amputation would be necessary. When I went to the hospital I was excused all duties immediately. I lay on my back for a couple of weeks before recovery. Nor has my leg ever been the same since. It is a miracle that I still have it.

When I came out of hospital this time I was very conscious of the way in which the atmosphere of the camp had changed. I had a feeling that somehow the mixture of orders, discipline, emotions and personal relationships, which held together the entire camp community, including the S.S., was disintegrating. The power from inside and outside the camp, which had seemed so formidable a year before, was now weakening. The life of the camp was no longer a relentless, inhuman machine; it had become a shambles.

This was apparent in preparations for the next S.3. The second S.3, with its appalling casualty rate, produced very little productive labour and the S.S. at the underground factory for which it was intended reported the fact to Berlin. They complained that the bulk of the men who reported to them were too weak to work. The S.S. in Berlin were furious at the waste of time and transport facilities involved, and made an enquiry into the method by which the personnel for the transport had been selected. They were not satisfied with the excuses made by the S.S. at Buchenwald. They made it clear that in future drafts of labour from Buchenwald must be made up of men capable of being worked for a reasonable length of time before they collapsed.

Having been on the carpet, the S.S. commandant at Buchenwald decided that he had better not make mistakes of this kind again. He gave orders that the next S.3 must include only first-class labour. It would be selected not by the prisoner hierarchy, but by the S.S. themselves, who would also supervise its embarkation and departure, so that there would be no last minute switchings. These preparations were kept secret from the Kapos.

The S.S. labour officer gave orders for a parade of all fit personnel. With every fit man under their eyes on the square, the S.S. staff walked around and selected about a thousand of the fittest looking men. These, it was then announced, would go on the draft. Such a selection of men naturally included a high percentage of the prisoner hierarchy. Dozens of Kapos, several block commanders and scores of their underlings and hangers-on, who had had double rations, good beds and the easiest work for years, were on the list. A wave of consternation shook the prisoner bosses and the whole camp was tense. Hundreds of prisoners smiled for the first time since they had been at Buchenwald—but only to themselves.

After the S.S. had made their selection, however, they left it to their headquarters clerks to prepare the nominal rolls. Some of these clerks in turn left the jobs to their clerks, who were prisoners. Once this became known there was a terrific burst of lobbying, threatening, cajoling and bribery. Before the transport left, many influential camp communists had been taken off the list and the names of other prisoners substituted. All the same, many of the leading camp communists had to go on the S.3 in the end. The fate to which they had consigned so many dying men was now overtaking them, when they were fit and well.

In some ways Buchenwald was a better place after this. One of the conditions of the prisoner bosses' success had been that they exercised their power behind the scenes as far as possible. But to save themselves from the third S.3 they had had to come out in the open. Their selfishness and ruthless self-interest had been exposed. Their failure to survive this draft unscathed only emphasised the success they had had at the expense of the rest of the prisoners on all previous occasions. The fact that their power, when the S.S. bothered to do their duty, had proved so limited, further diminished their hold upon the camp. From that time on the communist bosses lost a good deal of their authority.

This was not altogether a good thing. The vested interests and self-seeking of an apparently well-established prisoner hierarchy had preserved a kind of stability and order, psychological as well as physical. All that had now gone and the result was disintegration.

Between now and our liberation, a period of two months or so, Charles and I escaped being sent on transports several times. On one occasion I was limping back to the blockhouse after doing some light fatigue in the kitchen, when I saw a squad of Jewish prisoners being marched off to a transport from the block under the supervision of a Kapo. Among them was Charles. Any transport was highly dangerous, but to be included in a transport of Jews was a death sentence. Wherever they were said to be going, for whatever purpose, we knew by now that in fact the Jews would go to their death. Life was now cheaper than ever, food harder to come by. As the German armies were being pushed back, they had to evacuate more and more of their prisoners from outlying camps and re-incarcerate them in the more central places which remained secure. (When I arrived a year before, the number assigned to me was 21,521. Now there were prisoners numbered in the 80,000s.) Any opportunity of lessening the pressure on facilities and resources by liquidating a thousand Jews was obviously valuable.

My first foolish impulse was to rush to the cinema where the transport was assembling. At any moment its door would be locked on the victims. They would be released in the small hours of the next morning to be hounded like cattle on to the trucks. But fortunately I kept my head. I went to Rudolf and told him what I had seen.

He wasted no time. He made straight for the cinema. Charles, who told me afterwards what happened, was standing like a sheep wondering what was in store for him and waiting to be marched into the cinema. The bull-like Rudolf strode up to the Kapo, who was ticking off the names, and burst into a torrent of abuse.

'You fool, you bloody fool,' he bellowed. 'This one isn't a Jew . . .'

And roaring with rage, he seized my brother by the scruff of the neck and dragged him out of the ranks and flung him out into the square. Staggering, off balance, Charles seized his cue and hobbled off to his block. Rudolf swore at him and at the Kapo indiscriminately, blaming them equally for their stupidity. The Kapo stammered his apologies. Rudolf stalked off fuming and muttering, as though he had suffered a monstrous indignity.

My brother's life was saved in this fantastic, farcical, unreal moment, which seemed as though it had come out of a dream or a boy's adventure story. But the moment was real enough. So was Rudolf's courage and resourcefulness.

II

The likelihood of liberation came as no surprise to us. We were perfectly aware of the course of the war, and that the allies were approaching. We knew Germany could not last much longer. That the camp should fall to the allies was inevitable. But the dramatic and terrible question was: Should we survive to see it?

I think I can do no better than follow my journal day by day during this fatal period:

April 2

We expect our 'liberators' from one day to the other. They say that there is no question of evacuation of the camp. 'Sauckel would have given carte blanche to the commandant of the camp'—rumours fly wildly, though they are almost outdistanced by events. . . .

The death-rate is terrifying. Doctor Tallon has given me the official figures: January, more than two thousand; February, five thousand, six hundred; March, over five thousand. Incredible. Incredible also the grip of tuberculosis, particularly among the young. . . .

Yesterday there was a concert on the Appelplatz. A young Frenchman sang 'Ménilmontant', and it was transmitted by the camp radio! For the first time. I imagine the S.S. Commandant is trying to soothe us.

I am told that, while I was at the hospital, my friends had had news, by one of the Kapos of the S.S., of our poor dear Yves. It seems that he has a safe job at the Effecten-Kamer. Please

God, let that at least not be a rumour! In any case Michelin is dead, which I consider a crime, a voluntary and premeditated murder.

It seems that an S.S. said in Block 50: 'There's nothing to fear in the camp, except in the case of provocation on the part of the prisoners. On our part, in any case, there will be no provocation.' Significant.

April 3

Tonight we expect them to blow up the riding school—where the monstrosities took place in 41–42.

Block 46 was disbanded forty-eight hours ago and the archives destroyed. At Block 50 the Sturmbandführer has said goodbye. Panzer Faust guns have been installed in the miradors. The Kapo and prisoner chief at the crematorium have been hanged and the archives are burning. It seems, therefore, this evening, that things are coming to a head. No likelihood of evacuation, I hope. There could be only one disagreeable solution: the abandonment of the camp by the S.S. and a night bombing raid—which wouldn't leave many alive!

April 4

I am waiting for the morning Appel. It is not to be held till 9 o'clock. I wonder if that means evacuation? I pray God not! Still waiting for the Appel at 9.30.

I don't know why, but I feel there's something sinister about this late Appel. Also bread has been distributed for two days—one loaf for five.

Nevertheless the kitchen is working all right—which isn't a bad sign.

This morning, complete silence. It is a beautiful cold day. I went out about six o'clock to see Walter. Not an aeroplane in the sky, except for a few German fighters. And here we are, living through the last days probably, but they are by far the most anxious.

3.30 p.m. No Appel this morning. And when the air raid alert was over there was no question of an Appel. Lots of transports arriving. The camp must have grown by six or seven thousand; I imagine we must now be about forty thousand.

April 5

We are all waiting on the Appelplatz. There's a Jew hunt in the camp. From time to time one hears pistol shots and cries . . . S.3 has come back.

This evening, for the first time since I have been at Buchenwald, the Appel was held inside the blockhouses. It's true that there are about fifteen thousand new arrivals on the Appelplatz this evening. Poor wretches, in an incredible state of misery, and fighting among themselves. Extraordinary scenes. It seems that the S.S. are in a highly nervous state and are laying about them with truncheons. Apparently they were killing men who couldn't follow, for about one kilometre beyond the camp.

April 6

Dangerous situation in the camp. About forty-six prisoners —among whom are Neumeister, Kapo of the Schreibstube, the Kontrolleur Hauptmann, Kogon, Jan Robert (and six others from Block 50, all N.N.!), the Kapo of the Revier, the Kapo of 46 . . . and finally Bloch, the French aircraft builder (though I think this is an error)—have been called to Check Point 3, and have refused to go! This is a definite act of rebellion. (Note: As it turned out later, only Bloch went, and to everyone's surprise, came back safely.)

April 8

During the night of the 6–7, three S.S. came into our block, woke us and demanded who was ill or wounded. General consternation. Evidently this has to do with the evacuation of the camp. Are the sick and wounded to be executed? We have all got our bags ready.

Raymond Viguier, with Moriquand's agreement, has offered Charles and me a place at the hospital. We should go there this morning (I write during the night of 7–8 at 3.30 a.m. Charles and I have been taking it in turn on guard, so as to be able to warn of any attempt by the S.S. to surround the block and force us to leave at night).

We had to ask permission of Captain T.R. to take up the

places in the hospital. He said he saw nothing against it from his official point of view, that it was up to me to take the responsibility, that we might thus gain forty-eight hours, but that on the other hand it was perfectly possible that the hospital might be blown up.

Midday—I am lying beside Charles in the tuberculosis ward. There are a few other malingerers like us, mostly communists, except for Soudan, the Belgian minister, and Marie, deputy for Rouen. Saw Walter this morning, just before coming here —he is fairly optimistic.

12.15 p.m.—I was writing this when Rudolf came to tell me of the evacuation. All the blocks from 1 to 50 to report on the Appelplatz. A little later the situation becomes critical. Refusal of the block leaders to obey. S.S. confine prisoners to barracks; and immediately afterwards we think we hear cannon-fire. The situation is very dangerous and our lives hang by a thread. Panzer Faust and machine-guns, trained on the camp, may at any moment open fire on us.

Afternoon—I know nothing more. But it seems that some blocks cannot have been completely emptied, as there are still quite a lot of people about. The worst part is just waiting and not being able to do anything.

Our boots and clothes are rolled up under our heads and everything is ready for instant escape. Viguier told me that there is an underground shelter below this block where the Kapo of the hospital has been hiding ever since he was called to Check Point 3. If anything happens we shall go there. Of course if they set fire to the block we shall burn like rats; but at any rate it gives us a chance.

A charming little dog called Mauritz, a kind of dachshund with long, curly hair, has come into the ward. I can't imagine what he can live on. I expect he is as hungry as we are, although his tummy is so blown-up. I am horrified by the silence. Stertorous breathing from the dying. Their numbers have been inked on their thighs. Ripe for the crematorium. I find a little comfort in the presence of Charles; but the silence horrifies me. The Americans *must* arrive tonight or tomorrow, or else . . .!

Later—There is nothing else to do but write on this sinister day. What will become of us? . . . Charles and I have been amusing ourselves for the last two minutes—Mauritz runs like a mad thing round the ward, making a steeplechase across the dying, dragging behind him a rag bigger than he is, and worrying bits of straw that he found in a bolster! It's an odd mixture of comic and tragic, as Rudolf, who has a taste for that kind of thing, remarked.

Evening—A turn for the better. Incredible—the S.S. seem to have capitulated. They threatened to machine-gun the blocks, but finally did nothing. Although Rudolf says that twenty thousand men have already left Buchenwald others say that only five thousand have gone.

I have yesterday's figures: nine thousand Jews, of whom thirty-six were killed by the S.S. as they left camp—not too bad, considering. Perhaps we'll win through, after all. I imagine it's simply a question of holding out for another three or four days.

April 9

Viguier gave me more news last night. About five thousand have left from Blocks 10 and 14; and the greater part of my Block 26. Today another five or ten thousand are to go. At this rate the camp will be empty in four days, so we have a chance.

Yesterday Rudolf gave us twenty lumps of sugar—a diet for two—and this morning noodles. The stores of these 'seigneurs' are unlimited!

An air raid alert has been on for hours, and American planes are turning above us with an irritating mosquito-like persistence.

Thanks to the planes, the transports have not left. Five of our neighbours who have dysentery leave for Block 61. Their numbers are inked on their thighs. A death sentence. God be with them!

April 10

A day of drama. At eleven o'clock Rudolf announced that the total evacuation of the camp had been ordered. Now, at one o'clock, the radio announces to the Lager Altester I (Chief prisoner—Hans Heider of Trèves) that the transport must be ready to leave at four. Will the whole camp leave this evening? We ourselves will probably go tomorrow, unless they have other plans for us. In any case the situation is critical, and all we can do is to put ourselves in God's hands. The situation is so terribly dangerous. Charles is beside me, calm, and well rested.

April 11

We are still in Barrack 7 this morning. There are even seven newcomers; but this means nothing. Viguier told me yesterday that Horn has sent a note to the Commandant of the camp, invoking international law, and asking him to respect the hospital. I believe that out of four thousand sick, eight hundred are immovable, two thousand, five hundred transportable on stretchers; and seven hundred are more or less able to walk. An evacuation would therefore be a complete catastrophe for the sick.

We hear that Erfurt has fallen. Let's hope it's true, but even so it won't help much. We need to be surrounded to the north and the south, for all evacuation to be impossible! Only then can we have any reason to hope. Apparently there are still enough men left in the camp to make up a transport today. But even if it's not today, tomorrow is more than likely, unless the S.S. Lagerführer agrees to leave us here. It would be wisest for him as well as for us. But how can one hope for wisdom in this moment of panic? The artillery is certainly closer, but we hear very little aircraft activity for the moment. Though it wouldn't take long for planes to change the situation.

The camp and S.S. seem calm, although they fired a few shots yesterday.

I am writing in the middle of a Panzer alarm—the first. One hears firing from time to time from the machine-gun in the wood at the bottom of the camp. Russian soldiers were evacuated by road yesterday, but, three kilometers from Weimar, helped by American dive-bombing, nearly all escaped. Few killed, a few wounded. A wounded S.S. managed to get back here, and it was he who told the story. That's the news! Rudolf seems optimistic. Machine-gun fire coming from the left. Artillery

in front of us. Which makes me think that we have been by-
passed to the north-east by tanks and light infantry. Just now a
voice has roared an order over the radio which I never heard
before. 'All S.S. out of the Camp!' Now, complete silence. The
S.S. have marched up the alley by the hospital, taking all their
stuff, and all the horses. An S.S. who has lost a leg, mounted on
a grey horse, is the last to leave.

We are liberated. After a short fight outside the camp, machine-
gun fire was turned on the S.S. barracks. Then we heard the
groaning of the tanks. First wave, second wave; third and
fourth wave. Always machine-gun fire from below. The S.S.
in the miradors abandoned their posts. Three minutes later the
electrified cables were disconnected and over-run and the camp
made its first prisoners. From the breech of a gun of a disarmed
S.S. prisoner, I took an unfired cartridge (which I still have
today). Charles is annoyed because I don't want to wander
about the camp without any official job. The Russians are
drunk and ready for anything. It would be too stupid to get
oneself knocked off now. A moment ago Neumeister, who was
being searched for all over the camp three days ago, spoke on the
radio. This was followed by the B.B.C.'s French half-hour—
wonderful news of the war. Bremen, Hamburg, Brunswick,
Hanover, Thuringia, Coburg. Enormous advance of the English,
especially in north Germany. A soldier of de Gaulle's army,
good-looking, covered with brass, and pleasant (he has been
given a camp bodyguard, because he tried to give cigarettes to
the Russians, and was nearly mobbed), has just told us that the
French, Belgians and Luxembourgeois will be evacuated first.
The Russians, Poles, etc. will stay until the junction of the allies
with the Russians. Everything is very calm, and yet I am
exhausted—it is the sudden relief after all those hours of anxiety.
Thank God to have delivered us from all that horror and anxiety.

April 12

First day of liberty. But the Germans aren't far away, and
there might well be a counter-offensive—I didn't sleep much

last night! Disgusting day. International anti-fascist ceremony. Captain T. R. (who, as I said before, was a representative of the French prisoners in the camp) spoke in the name of the French; not one word of de Gaulle; not a word of our dead; two short words on the Americans; followed by paeans of praise of the Red Army. I am going to try to have Mass said on Sunday on the Appelplatz, with public absolution and communion.

One ought to be so happy. But all this is revolting. This morning I feared a counter-offensive by the Germans, but this evening I am almost sorry it didn't happen—it might have cleaned up some of this filth. It has just been announced on the radio that all the space around the camp is now occupied by American infantry. Appeal for discipline. Behaviour in the camp is lamentable. The Russians have tried to pillage the stores, so much so that a machine-gun has had to be put there. Potatoes stolen, etc. So shameful, so low! And when I think of our wretched comrades, dragging themselves along the roads eastwards, being massacred all along the way, and not a single word spoken of them at that ghastly meeting this morning.

April 13

I can't stop thinking of all those comrades of my Block 26, gone to an unknown fate on the roads of Germany. We have Raymond Viguier to thank, Charles and I, that we are still here. Without him, we might well have been dead by now.

Saw Jan Robert yesterday, who told me the magnificent story of Kogon. After he was called to Check Point 3 to be hanged, he got himself smuggled out of the camp in a packing case, dressed in the Luftwaffe uniform, with all the necessary papers. As soon as he was outside the camp, he made for the front, and was able to get across the lines and warn the Americans of our terrible situation. It is to him we all owe our lives.

The camp is now under American control. Just now all men with arms were ordered to report on the Appelplatz, also the members of the various national committees, so as to be presented to the American commandant. Apparently Patton's army has so far come across only 'liquidated' camps. It seems that the roads are littered with corpses, and for us at Buchenwald, the liquidation order was received an hour too late, and was received—irony!—by the chief prisoner.

Later—I am so afraid for our comrades who set out on the roads eastward. I don't think there can be much doubt about the fate of most of them. Fearful also for uncle Bernard, of whom I am particularly thinking. Fearful for all of them. Above all I fear the realisation of Hitler's prophecy: 'I will pull down the world in my fall!'

The news is fantastic. The English especially have made a big advance. I don't suppose the war can last much longer.

April 15

We can still hear artillery, but I think the situation is much improved since the 12th, when the front was only twenty-five yards wide, twenty miles from its base—as one of the allied officers told me. He confirmed that the Americans thrust out an arm expressly to save us. Also it is now certain that the order for the liquidation of the prisoners was given; and apparently the one who gave it (the police chief at Weimar) is now in the hands of the Americans. I was also told that a flame-throwing party was actually on its way to the camp, when intercepted by the Americans.

I must stop. My head aches too much, and I am too tired.

The S.S. had marched out of Buchenwald as though rehearsing for a victory parade on the Wilhelmstrasse. The Americans came in looking like tramps. They seemed to wear any garments that took their fancy; anything, in fact, except uniform. They had camouflage on their helmets, they were unshaven and unwashed, and they had cigarettes and cigars in their mouths. It was impossible to distinguish officers from men.

Those prisoners who could walk now left their huts and went out on to the parade ground. We noticed that, tough as the Americans were, they quailed when they saw us. We must have been a terrible sight. Their manner towards us was peculiar. They looked at us and spoke to us in a curious way, like an ordinary person might behave towards people they knew to be mentally ill, idiot children, cretins. They seemed half frightened, half suspicious of us. They behaved as though they felt that we were not really altogether human; and I suppose we were not. There we were, gaunt, cadaverous, hysterical, jumping and leaping, chattering and grimacing, many of us half demented with joy.

The first few days of liberation were by no means pleasant. It was not only that the Americans regarded us, and indeed had to treat us, as sub-human, and that we felt this and resented it. They had no idea, quite naturally, of how to treat men who had been in captivity for many years. Their very generosity was a source of trouble. They distributed their jam and meat rations with the utmost liberality. Hundreds of prisoners fell like wolves on the food. Most of them became ill and dozens died. Their digestive systems could not cope with such a diet.

They made another mistake, natural enough but much more serious, which caused great bitterness among the prisoners. They knew nothing about the internal politics of the camp and, so far as they were concerned, everybody in the camp was in the same category. To them they were all decent men, victims of the Nazis. In consequence they appointed all kinds of murderers, swindlers and black-marketeers to preside over the dissolution of the camp. These men helped themselves to all the wealth that had been accumulated by the Kapos. Others, who should have been brought to book for their behaviour to thousands of fellow prisoners, were allowed to leave the camp untouched.

However, these Americans were not trained for the exacting job of liberating concentration camps. They came to Buchenwald by chance, because they were the advance patrols of General Patton's army. They were paratroopers, not occupation troops. They did their best.

I was in any case too ill to be much of a judge of what happened. Within a few hours of the Americans' entry into the camp I was in bed in the hospital. This time, however, I was being looked after by a medical officer, who, if over-burdened with patients, at any rate could be trusted not to liquidate any of them. The longed-for day had done nothing to strengthen me. If anything, it had had the opposite effect. I lay listless on my bed without any desire to move, much less to leave the camp. Many others had this same reaction. I suppose that once the tensions which had kept us alive were relaxed, we had temporarily nothing to live for. My mind was empty and there was no feeling left in me. I was perfectly conscious of what was going on around me and within me, and that was all. I thought of my mother and father, of my home, of the roof showing among the trees, of the leafy lanes surrounding it, visions which had buoyed me up for years in my moments of despair. But now I thought of them without any feeling whatsoever, I knew my brother was not far away, but I did not bother to go and see him. For five days I lay like this perceiving everything but feeling nothing. I think that if I had suddenly been told that the S.S. had reoccupied the camp and that I was down for another transport, I would not have batted an eyelid. Or perhaps, indeed, that *would* have brought me to life.

After five days I remember registering the thought that I should be making enquiries about being repatriated. With no enthusiasm whatsoever, no interest even, I got up and walked over to the main watch-tower where the Americans had set up their H.Q. On my way to the watch-tower I bumped into Professor R., a member of a famous family of doctors.

'When you get back to France, my boy,' he said, 'you must spend six months in a sanatorium before you do anything else. You must take care of yourself. You must get yourself properly rehabilitated before you start your normal life.' I did not take his advice. It was a very great mistake.

As I entered the watch-tower, now staffed by French troops as well as American, the first man I saw was a colonel who had been one of my schoolteachers when I was sixteen. He did not recognise me, but when I spoke to him he knew me at once. He was well informed about the fortunes of the underground and gave me a great deal of news about my old friends. He was extremely kind to me. He was very comfortably billeted in Weimar in a house which had belonged to the Nazis, and he suggested that I leave the camp at once and spend a week or two with him until I felt fit to travel. I still had no wish to go home, no wish to do anything. It was wonderful to find somebody who would make up my mind for me. That evening I went back to his house. It was my first night of freedom for four and three-quarter years, and it felt completely unreal, like an unexciting dream. I remember that for dinner we ate some ham and an egg and that one glass of wine made me tight.

A couple of weeks went by. I still had no desire to go home or indeed to do anything but allow myself to be borne on by the flow of everyday events. I would have lounged around in his flat almost indefinitely, if Colonel L. had not one day brought back with him another French officer, who had come to fetch me. Richard Broad, the British officer whom I had helped to escape from occupied France, was now military attaché at the British Embassy in Paris. He had discovered that I was in Buchenwald and he had sent a message to have me brought back.

I think I must pause at this point to recount an incident which throws a light on the extraordinary, stubborn heroism of my father's character. Richard Broad had discovered that it was possible to buy the life of a prisoner at Buchenwald. He went to my uncle, Jean de Caraman Chimay, and very generously they offered to supply, between them, this vast sum. Aware though my father was of the appalling conditions and dangers of Buchenwald, he refused to accept it, on the grounds that my future would have been impossible had I been bought out of the camp. He was absolutely right, though it must have been a terrible decision for a father to take. For this foresightedness, as for the generosity of my uncle and my friend, I shall be eternally grateful.

Colonel L., having consulted with his medical officers, was opposed to my going back by air. He was convinced my health would not stand it. The plane therefore went without me and I was sent off in a car with my brother. Even this was a strain. I collapsed at Reims and had to rest for a couple of days before I could go on. I was taken straight to my parents' flat. Half-way up the six flights of stairs I began to tremble violently. Then my father came out on to the landing and down the stairs to meet me. I embraced my parents, still feeling that everything was unreal, experiencing only a sense of anti-climax. Then I went straight to bed.

For several days I lay in bed in a state of lethargy. A curious disease afflicted my legs. There seemed nothing physically wrong with them but suddenly they became hypersensitive, so that the slightest contact with anything brought on intense pain. I could not bear even the weight of the sheets upon them. A framework of arches had to be made so that the bed linen should not touch them.

As some degree of feeling had begun to flow again in my mind, I felt a kind of antagonism towards the world around me. It was as though I felt that I could never enter it or be part of it again, and the feeling made me resentful. Everybody and everything seemed to emphasise my 'differentness'. I almost wanted to be back in Buchenwald where I fitted in.

I remember going to church for the first time. As I entered the crowded church, some of those already seated moved up to make room. I felt very aware of the fact that I seemed very different from them. My head was still shaven, of course; my cheeks were sunken, my eyes glowed like candles in the sockets of a skull. I certainly *was* different from them. But I hated to be made to feel so, and I hated them for doing it to me.

And yet I wanted to be different. I did not want to identify myself, or be identified, with the life of the France around me. I wanted to go on living the life of the camp.

I felt this come to a head when I heard about my sister's marriage. Soon after my brother and I arrived home in late April, we learned that our sister was to be married in a few days' time.

They were married at our Parisian parish church. I remember going to the church, but when I reached the door, I could not go inside. I told my parents to continue without me and I would remain outside. I sat on a chair in the garden at the side of the church, and prayed for the happiness of my sister and her husband-to-be. As soon as the ceremony was over, I walked back alone to my parents house, for I was unequal to joining the reception.

At the time my mind was still so weak and confused that I did not understand what was going on. Now I do. The everyday life of the outside world was in such stark contrast to the life I had lived for five years that I simply could not take it. The life the ordinary

Frenchman was living seemed sham, trivial, absurd, compared with life in the camp. The way of the normal world was an insult and a mockery to those who had lived and died in Buchenwald.

Nobody, naturally enough, wanted to hear of Buchenwald. France's spirit had been crushed by the Occupation. She was still at war. Men and women around me wanted to forget the past, and much of the present as well. They had had their own tragedies and they did not want to be reminded of other people's. I could not help feeling resentment that nobody seemed to care about what we had gone through.

However, as soon as I was physically strong enough, I myself was trying to forget Buchenwald. Instead of taking my old friend's advice and spending six months in a sanatorium, I spent just about the same amount of time in a mad round of pleasure.

The same thing happened to several of my friends. Once the initial feeling of lassitude had gone and something like normal physical health had returned, one became aware of a feeling of a kind of starvation. We wanted to have good food, good wine, parties, women, and all of it in excess. It was not appetite, but a kind of obsessive greed, which was neurotic, compulsive, and endless. The more you had, the more you wanted. I think that at the bottom of this mad complex was a fear that life had passed one by because of Buchenwald, that one could never enjoy food, and music, and laughter and women again. We wanted to try to prove to ourselves that life would be as full for us as ever, and that we were as capable as ever of enjoying it. If we were refused anything, we acted like spoiled children. I remember P., a great friend of mine, who had been a great Resistance fighter, and is today a well-known man in public life. He went almost mad with anger one night in my car, because the girl he was with did not respond to his advances. Rich, handsome and attractive as he was, he could have picked up twenty prettier girls in an hour. But because this one had said no, he was beside himself. If I had not restrained him I think he would have thrown her out of the car.

With others of my friends drink and drugs took their toll. It was the same irrational race to catch up with pleasure. In my case I yearned to make up to myself the youth I had lost. I wanted to forget that I was old and weak. So I married a girl of seventeen, really only because she was young and healthy and full of life. And, of course, there was no happiness in it and inevitably it failed.

It is extraordinary to look back and see how so many men, who had withstood the physical and moral trials of captivity, disintegrated within a few weeks of beginning to live a life of so-called liberty. Perhaps their whole moral personality had become mysteriously transformed to face the challenge of the camp, and, when that challenge had been withdrawn, it proved incapable of resuming its normal, lower form. All I know is that often when it became hardest of all for men to behave like decent human beings they spread their wings and rose to great heights; and when the strains and temptations were removed, they sank into the mud.

In their heart of hearts they may have felt, as I did, that in its way it was the life of the camp that was the true life, the life that bore witness to what really counted in humanity, the spirit. The life to which they had now returned was a sham. They could no longer take it seriously, behave as though *its* values were the ones that counted; but they had no wish to challenge it, attack or improve it, and make the great majority who believed in it disturbed and unhappy. So they tried to escape from the contradiction, by every means from sex to drink and drugs. And the drugs and drink killed many of them, as, I suspect, many of them had hoped.

This for me is the first lesson of the camp—that it made beasts of some men and saints of others. And the second lesson of the camp is that it is hard to predict who will be the saint and who the beast when the time of trial comes. Men famous and honoured in pre-war France, regarded as natural leaders, showed neither spirit nor authority in the camp. Other men, of seemingly mediocre brains and character, who would never have been noticed in ordinary times, shone out like beacons as the true leaders. Under the stresses and strains imposed by life in the camp, only one thing prevailed—strength of character. Cleverness, creativeness, learning all went down; only real goodness survived.

Sooner or later weakness of fibres was revealed in a man, and sooner or later it destroyed him. Self-discipline was essential, and this is the basis of character. For instance, the question of the open fire: it had been very tempting, especially in the cold winter nights, to go and lie by the open braziers in our blockhouse. But it was fatal. A man began by lying some distance from the fire, on the outer ring. But the fire drew like a magnet. He would go closer to the flames, until finally he would get as near as he possibly could. The contrast between the heat of the fire at night and the cold of the Appel in the morning was too much for these poor human frames. It was only a matter of time before it killed them. The fact that every prisoner knew this did not prevent a great many from succumbing. If a prisoner began habitually to leave his bunk in the night and lie down to sleep on the floor around the fire, you knew that he had decided, even if he had not faced his own decision, that death was preferable to discomfort.

As I write about the temptation of the fire, which symbolises all the temptations of the camp, I think of P., a famous scientist who was among us. P. had begun the downhill path by selling his margarine ration to obtain cigarettes. He could not afford this deficiency in fat, as he well knew, and it became necessary for him to obtain heat from the fire. Gradually P. moved from the outside circle of the sleepers to the centre. Every night he got a little nearer. For a week or so he slept as close to it as he could get. And then, because he had failed to discipline his craving for cigarettes, he died.

It seemed to me that those men displayed most character who had the capacity for living on their own and that these men possessed something which is easiest described as religion, faith, or devotion. I saw that leadership exercised by Christians. I saw it in communists too. It was displayed by people who had no religious faith or political creed in any formal sense, but who still had some inner core which gave them a belief in life, when the rest of us were lost.

The camp showed me that a man's real enemies are not ranged against him along the borders of a hostile country; they are often among his own people, indeed, within his own mind. The worst enemies are hate, and greed, and cruelty. The real enemy is within.

186